Folk Tales and Fables

Of

The Gambia

Volume 3

By

Sukai Mbye Bojang

Published in 2012 by Educational Services

ISBN 978-9983-901-09-2

Acknowledgements

I am deeply grateful to Mrs. Sarjo Jarju and her husband, Ebou Camara of Sibanor village for the stories from the Jola tribe featured in this book. Mr. Samba Mbye of Bakoteh filled in the blank parts of the story of Boppi Jerreh that had been narrated to me in the past by my late maternal grandmother, Yai Marie Joof. She had obtained her story from her late father, Baka Chorro Joof who was a captain of a cutter. The stories about 'Mai's nianyaa get stolen' as well as 'the birds migrate' are some of the favourite stories of my mother, Mrs. Joanna Mbye and her late maternal grandmother, Fatou Sanneh. Mrs. Mbye had been very instrumental in enlivening these stories.

I wish to thank the famous storyteller and

griot, Mr. Dembo Conteh of Brikama for narrating the story of 'the six children of the world'. I appreciate Ya Satou Njie, a native of Ballangharr who now resides in Sinchu Alagie for narrating the Wollof story, 'Kumba Ndaba marries Jeggan Touray'.

I am deeply grateful to all those who narrated the stories. I recorded, translated and reworked all of the tales to ensure interesting reading.

I also appreciate the immense work put into the editing, layout and design of this book. I thank all those who contributed in one way or another towards enriching it.

Introduction

This selection of stories was gathered from the Wollof, Mandingo and Fula tribes.

The story of 'Boppi Jerreh' has been much narrated by the Wollof people of Banjul and the fisher folk of Barra and its neighbourhood from time immemorial. It showed the immense power of the genii living near one of the islands in the northern part of North Bank region, Dog Island. In the past, many people in Banjul and the Niumis earned their living as fishermen. They travelled the length of the country by boat on the navigable river returning home to narrate captivating stories about the genii at Bambatenda and Dog Island.

Although the tale about the 'six children of the world' seemed to discuss creation, it also brings out the moral virtues that are so treasured by our people.

The Wollof story, 'Kumba Ndaba marries Jeggan Touray' shows how the institution of marriage fosters kinship ties. It also brings out the immense importance attached to moral values such as devotion and care to parents, respect for elders and service to the community.

The stories gathered from the Jola tribe were: 'Elephant, Hyena, Snake and Tiger agree to separate', 'a feather for a goat', 'Mr. Hyena and Mr. Hare live together in one home' as well as 'the bird and the lion fight for a beautiful girl'. The tales were based on the occupational lives of women, one of which was rearing small ruminants, the deep appreciation of nature and the traditional practice of consulting soothsayers before embarking on any major initiative. The moral lessons of the tales portray the shared values of many virtues among the people of The Gambia.

Content
Page

Chapter One

Boppi Jerreh

Baka Chorro, the captain of the boat, Rougie announced to the merchants in Banjul that he was planning his next trip to the provinces and would leave in a week's time. Three days after his announcement, people started to come singly or in groups to his house to register and pay for their journeys. They were going to different towns and would get off either in Albadarr, Bambatenda or the destination port of Dandimayo.

Small traders in Banjul like Batch and Bamusa bought bamboo and Kirinting from the provinces for resale in the city and its environs. Baka had one of the biggest boats in the city. It could take over twenty-five passengers and ten tonnes of assorted goods and luggage. During the groundnut-buying season, children of well-known traders stationed in the provinces such as Balingho, Dandimayo and Kuntaur travelled in his boat to spend their holidays with their parents.

Baka had never taken any of his young children, teenage nieces and nephew for a trip on his boat. They had only sat in the boat whilst it was docked. This time, though, Baka had a surprise for them. A few days before he was to set sail, he called his teenage nieces and nephew Hujeja, Ndella and Massireh to his room. He had finished his lunch and was reclining on his day bed for his afternoon siesta.

The three children entered nervously. They were only summoned together to their uncle's living quarters when they did something wrong. They could not remember committing any offence over the last few hours or days that could anger the experienced sea captain. As they approached his verandah they felt the usual surges of adrenalin. Their knees weakened as they cautiously entered his room and meekly greeted him. They examined his expressionless face for a clue of what was coming. They could read nothing. They therefore took their seats on the small bamboo stools at the far end of the room and waited for him to speak.

Baka looked at each of them in turn as they sat down. He sensed their suspense. He suspected that they were expecting the usual firm warning relating to some misconduct. He was amused but turned away to hide a grin. He paused for some time before addressing them thus:

"Come here, my young ones. Bring your stools nearer to me. Why do you look so timid? You've done nothing wrong. There's something that I've been meaning to tell you and I think that today is opportune. I have been toying with an idea which might be of interest to you."

2

Baka paused for some time. He could feel the positive change in the youngsters' attitudes. They became relaxed, attentive and curious. After a while, he continued:

"I am sure you are aware that some of your friends will be travelling with me to the provinces to spend their holidays with their parents. I will be leaving in a few days' time. I thought that.... you...can..."

Baka Chorro's last sentence was drowned in the midst of Massireh's excited claps. He stood up and cupped his mouth. Then he put his hands down and repossessed his seat. He looked at his siblings. There were wide smiles on their faces. In unison they turned to their uncle, speechless but putting on adoring smiles. Although earlier they did not wait for the completion of their uncle's sentence, they assumed that they knew what he wanted to say. Massireh's impulsive clap confirmed that at times they could predict their uncle's words. They were elated. Unconsciously, they dragged their stools even closer to his daybed. They wanted to hear more. Baka then continued:

"I know that you are now old enough to go to sea with me and it is about time that I gradually expose you to life in other parts of our country. Therefore, I intend to take you along with me to Dandimayo. You will see or go past places such as Boppi Jerreh, Albadarr, Johe, Bambatenda and Dandimayo. However, I intend to make three stops: Albadarr,

Bambatenda and Dandimayo. I want you to get used to travelling by sea and meeting people from different backgrounds. Travelling by sea is the quickest way to go to some of our provincial towns.

The river is navigable and you will experience a completely different journey compared to travelling by road. Once you get used to river transportation, you will quickly overcome seasickness. I have some mentholated mints, which will help you with dizziness at sea. You can talk to your friends, Banja, Dodou, Ma Awa and Bintu about their experiences in travelling by boat and living in an environment different from Banjul. They have been spending their holidays with their father, Abdou Wally at Balingho every year. I'm sure you'll enjoy the trip."

The three teenagers listened politely whilst their uncle spoke. They were already imagining the boat trip through the famous places he mentioned. They had never been outside Banjul so they knew very little about the countryside. Some of their friends joked about their lack of exposure. They were happy to have this golden opportunity to explore and then return home to narrate and share their experiences of provincial towns with their friends. Massireh spoke on behalf of his siblings.

"Uncle Baka, you don't know what you have done for us. We are overwhelmed by this good and pleasing news. Our friends used to tease us about our ignorance of places outside Banjul. This trip will be an eye opener for us. From hence we will be able to contribute in discussions about other people and places in this country. As you suggested, we will confide in our friends, Dodou, Banja, Ma Awa and Bintu. We are sure that seasickness will not be a major concern. Our friends will tell us what to do to avoid it. How long are we going to stay away?"

"We will be away for at least ten days. I usually spend between two to five days in each port to offload goods and passengers as well as seek new ones for the onward journey. For instance, when we are going to Dandimayo, my first stop will be Albadarr and then Bambatenda. Some people will get off there so that they can continue their journeys by road to other towns in the north bank of the country. I'll spend two to five days in Albadarr in order to get some passengers and goods bound for the central part of the country. Only a few hours is spent at Bambatenda before we proceed. We'll spend at least five days in Dandimayo. I always make sure that the boat is full before we depart. Dandimayo is a big trading post. You'll like this busy town. People from other towns and villages join my boat in order to come down to Albadarr and Banjul. I don't want to tell you everything about the voyage, scenery and life in other places. I want you to discover these parts of the country for yourselves. That way, you'll appreciate and learn about your environment. Now, run to your aunt, Lissa. She'll help you to prepare for the journey." Baka Chorro concluded.

The children got up to leave. One after the other, they lovingly gave tight and loving hugs to their uncle. With the close body contacts, the teenagers felt the well-developed chest muscles of their famous uncle. He held each of them very close to himself. Although he was not ostentatious about his feelings, he loved them dearly. He had been their guardian since his beloved sister, Lolly Ndoye died prematurely of a severe headache. At the time, all three children were under seven years old. They had grown up as an integral part of his family. He was their only parent. He regarded them as not only his nieces and nephew but also his children, an integral part of his nuclear family.

Lolly Ndoye was Baka's only sister and best friend. Their mother had the two of them with their father who had fourteen other children with his many wives. Baka lost contact with his half brothers and sisters when his father divorced their mothers. They left their father's home never to return. Thus the death of Lolly Ndoye transformed Baka into a lonely man. However, he was blessed with a good wife with whom he had three very young children. His nieces and nephew together with his loving wife and biological children were his joy.

On leaving their uncle's house, Hujeja, Ndella and Massireh rushed straight to their aunt's living quarters. They could not contain their excitement. They talked simultaneously to Lissa about the news they received from Uncle Baka. Although her husband had secretly explained everything to her, she did not show any foreknowledge of the news. She listened and readily joined in their thrill. They told her that they were going to keep quiet about their envisaged trip until two days before their departure. Then they would tell their closest friends.

Two days before their departure, Baka's protégés told their friends, Dodou, Banja, Ma Awa and Bintu about the surprise trip that their uncle had sprung on them. The youths were thrilled. This was going to be their first sea journey together. Banja, Dodou, Ma Awa and Bintu agreed to give their friends some tips about travelling by sea since they were embarking on their maiden journey. They were used to sea voyage for they visited their parents annually at Balingho to spend part of their holidays. They had invited Massireh, Hujeja and Ndella to spend time with them at Balingho. The latter had accepted the open invitation, which was yet to materialise. Perhaps, the invitation to Balingho would happen very soon since Uncle Baka believed that his protégés were matured enough to travel to the provinces. They would soon move to another level whereby they could travel with their friends to spend part of their holidays in Balingho.

The seven friends discussed about the trip. They wanted the time to fly. The boys decided to surprise Uncle Baka by helping to paddle the boat. They spent the rest of the period working out. They did one hundred pushups every three hours. They were in a hurry to build firmer arm muscles. They were resolved to show that they were useful by helping the sailors to row for long distances.

Lissa and her nieces were very busy during the evening before the journey preparing food that the travellers would eat whilst away. Hujeja and Ndella prepared the Mbudakeh whilst Lissa fried a lot of bonga and red snapper fish. The fried fish were well done so that they would stay long. Lissa also prepared well-fried pepper, onions and fresh tomatoes that would be eaten with the fish. The women finished their cooking at dusk. They took some of the food and served it for the family dinner. Then they covered the rest with a white meshed cotton cloth and allowed it to cool.

The boat was to set sail by nine o' clock the next morning. All travellers were expected to be on board an hour earlier. This would allow the captain and his sailors to ensure that other unaccompanied goods were well packed. Baka left for the wharf after an early breakfast of chourah gerteh porridge and sour milk at seven o' clock. Massireh, Ndella and Hujeja left fifteen minutes later. They carried their luggage and the cooked food to the wharf. They wanted to arrive in good time so that they could help their uncle with the other passengers and their belongings.

When they arrived, their uncle and his men were already helping the early travellers to board the boat. The teenagers entered and packed their luggage under the supervision of Uncle Baka. Then they went to the wharf so that they could help the elderly and women travelling with small children to board. Dodou, Banja, Ma Awa and Bintu joined their friends in good time to help the rest of the travellers. They were all eager. This maiden journey together must be worthwhile so that Uncle Baka would allow his protégés to travel next time with their friends to Balingho.

Travellers were punctual because Baka was very strict about time. When the last passengers boarded, Baka, the sailors, his nephew, nieces and their friends went into the boat. The young friends were happy that they proved helpful. They saw the men at the wharf waving their hands, making signs and shouting to the sailors as the rope that kept the boat at dock was released. The boat started to glide slowly on the water. It was an exhilarating experience for Ndella, Hujeja and Massireh.

The winds were gentle and the boat was moving with the tide. People sat on the deck to enjoy the view of the calm waters of the tributary lined on both sides by thick, green, leafy mangroves. Oysters covering the roots and trunks of the mangroves brightly shone under the gentle morning sun. The leaves and branches of the mangroves however, escaped the clutches of the oysters. The adornment of the mangroves on both sides of the water enriched the vegetation. Rows of well-lined thick mangroves stretched as far as the eye could see. The tributary meandered as it followed the mangroves to join the river. The scenery was fascinating.

The boat smoothly sailed through the waters and with it the low buzz of conversation grew louder. Passengers became more confident of a smooth journey and ended their quiet prayers. They pointed to landmarks of the city such as Denton Bridge, the oil mill at Saaro, the State House and the Port Authority. Dodou could not resist the urge to lower his hand to touch the calm clear sea green waters near Wharfi Njaago. There was a lot of activity at the wharf. Small fishing canoes rocked from side to side on the waters unattended. Their captains and sailors loitered on the wharf as they struggled with full yellow twenty-litre containers to their canoes. They had obtained fuel for their expeditions for fish and shrimps down the river.

From their boat, Bintu could count ten idle canoes while another three had fishermen on board examining their fishing nets. The excited youngsters in Baka's boat watched the movements at the wharf with fascination. Baka's protégés did not realise that they would travel quite a distance before seeing activity of this sort.

The conversation in the boat was light. Passengers discussed about the different types of canoes bearing familiar names and sizeable boats anchored in the waters. They tried to establish the owners. There was a particular white boat with tinted glasses and communication equipment that caught special attention. Some of the passengers revealed that they had never seen such a sport boat. There were low whispers as regards the owner. Massireh overheard a senior female passenger saying quietly she understood that a rich Lebanese merchant owned the sport boat.

Baka and his men went past the myriad of boats and canoes to join the River Gambia. A novice traveller would not even notice that the boat had left the tributary and entered the river. The tide was low and the gentle wind blew fluttering the shawls of the women in the boat. The sun was gradually moving towards the west to reach overhead. The low hum of conversation became intermittent. All around the travellers, there was water, water, everywhere.

Baka asked his assistant, Ndeneh to tell all passengers that they would descend to the bottom as soon as they approached boom mi Beran Sirrah. Massireh was curious. He moved closer to Dodou and Banja and then whispered:

"What is happening? Why do we have to go down the hole? What is boom mi Beran Sirrah?"

Dodou smiled. Banja was the one who responded by asking his friend a question.

"Did your uncle not explain to you about boom mi Beran Sirrah?"

Massireh and his sisters were contented with a promise from Dodou. They knew that he would keep his word. They travelled for fifteen minutes, all of them very quiet. Then they noticed that the boat was taking a detour. It was moving away from land with a lot of trees that could be seen from afar. The front part of the land was shaped like the head of a dog. Ndeneh started to help the women and children descend to the bottom of the ship. The elderly men were next. The youths were allowed to descend last. Ndeneh and the other sailors joined them. As if by common agreement, everyone was quiet. Not even the babies cried. It seemed there was an unspoken conspiracy of silence. The frequent travellers did not betray if they had knowledge of what was happening.

The hole was dark and overcrowded. It was getting difficult to breathe. There was only the occasional light breeze that blew down. The faces of people shone from the beads of sweat. Their clothes stuck on their bodies. It was hot inside. Yet no one dared complain. They all waited. How would they know that they could resume their seats on the deck? Ndella wondered. She was not a small person and felt the heat unbearable.

The boat continued to move in the same direction for sometime. Then it felt as if it was changing its course. It turned towards the left as if heading towards the stretch of land. Ndeneh and his fellow sailors stood up. They helped women, children and elderly men go up the narrow steps to the deck. One could easily sense the relief among the passengers. Ndella, Hujeja, Ma Awa and Bintu ascended before their brothers. The young boys were the last to go up. When they regained their seats, Dodou, true to his word started to explain:

"Beran Sirrah is a genii who lives in the waters in front of Boppi Jerreh. He is elderly with a very long grey beard. Some say he has many wives and one hundred children. He has lived at Boppi Jerreh for hundreds of years. Genii are said to live longer than men. Beran Sirrah is very jealous. Whenever he sees a boat going near his area, he thinks that the captain has fallen in love with one of his wives. Therefore, in order to prevent a chance meeting between the captain and one of his women, he pulls the boat down as what happens in the Bermuda Triangle that is located in Central America near the Bahamas, Caribbean and the Straits of Florida in the United States. Boom mi Beran Sirrah is the dangerous undercurrent where the genii quietly waits for his victims."

Boat avoiding Boppi Jerreh

The young friends were quiet after Dodou's story.
Hujeja and Ndella were afraid and worried by what
they heard. Their uncle was a sea captain. They did not
want any mishap to befall him. They had never heard
the story. It was new to them. Yet Dodou did not
explain why they all had to go down the hole. Hujeja
enquired:

"Why did all the passengers have to go down the hole
except Uncle Baka?

Dodou looked at Hujeja in the eye and replied:

"For that, you'll have to ask your uncle. I wasn't on the
deck with him. How will I know why he didn't descend
and what he was doing?"

Massireh and his sisters decided that they would look for the opportune time to ask him more about the story of Beran Sirrah.It was not long before Baka's boat docked at Albadarr in late evening. Five passengers descended. Baka was very lucky this time. Four women with their babies came to reconfirm their intention to travel with him. The unaccompanied cargo had been neatly piled on the wharf in seven old fifty-kilo bags of sugar. The sailors helped the labourers to pack the goods in the boat. Since the winds were too strong and dusty they decided to spend the night in Albadarr. They would set sail again the next morning. Uncle Baka's friend, Bambo had a travellers' lodge that could easily accommodate all the passengers.

The next morning passengers trooped to the boat very early to board. There was no time to be wasted. The weather was nice and the sky was cleared of the dust of the previous evening. The captain hoped to get to the destination in good time. Thus he and his men arrived at the boat earlier than the passengers for inspection and preparations to sail.

The rest of the journey was not very eventful. Banja pointed out Johe, which was renamed James Island by the British colonialists to Massireh, Ndella and Hujeja. They had all learnt about the history of the slave trade and how many able bodied Gambians were taken to that island as slaves in preparation for a journey to distant lands where they worked in sugar plantations. They easily recognised the well-built fort with the armory mounted on a raised platform. The place was deserted. Banja observed:

"It's a pity that no one lives in Johe. If the place was made habitable for people, we will be able to preserve our history better. There are people living in the former slave fort of Goree in Senegal. That's why the place is well preserved. It attracts a lot of tourists. That helps the Senegalese economy."

"You know, I agree with you. A place is best taken care of when it is habitable. People in this area should be allowed to set up homes in Johe. Look at the way that the sea is eroding the land. Very soon, there'll be nothing left of the island," Bintu concurred.

The conversation died down as Johe faded in the distance. The boat avoided the nets that were thrown about to catch shrimps. They were of various sizes. The fishermen were nowhere to be seen. They had installed their nets and would return later to gather their catch. This was something new to Hujeja, Massireh and Ndella.

They had never thought that different methods were employed in catching fish and shrimps. They peered through the water hoping to catch glimpses of the shrimps in the small closely knitted nets. They marvelled at the multiple uses of the recycled yellow plastic twenty-litre containers. Massireh noted that the fishermen carried both empty and full containers in their canoes. To him, fishermen were a group that was good in recycling. They made multiple uses of these containers.

Massireh, Dodou and Banja ensured that they did not spend their time with their sisters all the time. They would shuttle between assisting Uncle Baka and his men and chatting with their sisters.

The journey was quick and smooth with the new travellers encountering very little problems. They did not have the feared seasickness and thoroughly enjoyed the company.

Banja, Dodou, Ma Awa and Bintu recognised that they were sailing through fresh water. It was a sign that they had entered the tributary that would soon take them to Bambatenda. They told their friends that they were approaching their destination. Banja warned them that they would shortly have to go down the hole for a brief period. When they were three hundred metres away from Bambatenda, the captain commanded all passengers and sailors to go down the hole. They complied. This time they were there for less than ten minutes when they were led up again to the deck. The young friends pretended as if nothing had happened. They did not discuss it.

Hujeja, Massireh and Ndella were saddened when the shores of Dandimayo became more visible. Their friends, Banja, Dodou, Bintu and Ma Awa were leaving them to go to Balingho by road. The boat docked at Dandimayo in the early evening. The friends hugged each other goodbye and left.

Uncle Baka informed his nieces and nephew that the number of passengers he could muster for the return journey would dictate the length of their stay in Dandimayo. They would not go back to Banjul together since Banja, Dodou, Bintu and Ma Awa were going to spend a month in Balingho.

After all the passengers had left the boat, Baka, his men, nephew and nieces cleaned it. They gathered their luggage and headed for the trading post of Njugga. Baka's friend was the biggest groundnut trader in Dandimayo. He had a big compound with many guest rooms. He was known for his hospitality in the whole of Saloum. Baka was a very close friend and Njugga reserved special rooms for him and his men.

He had told him that he intended to visit with his protégés when next he journeyed to Dandimayo. Thus Njugga expected the three youths who would share the same rooms as his own children. He had been used to chatting with his friend, Baka until very late. He did not want anything to change it as he looked forward to news from Banjul. Njugga's children openly welcomed their guests. They ate and chatted until very late at night when the lights were put off. They settled down with plans to explore the town on the following day.

The planned five-day break in Dandimayo was a good holiday for Hujeja, Massireh and Ndella. They strolled through the town of Dandimayo and met some of the friends of Njugga's children. Uncle Baka too was more relaxed and his loud laughs were frequently audible to the children. His protégés decided that they would wait for the right time to ask him more about Boppi Jerreh. They had the opportunity on the fourth day of their visit. The sun had not even ascended halfway on the sky when Uncle Baka wandered to the verandah where the youths were brewing some local tea, Mborr Mborr. Although he knew that the two sets of children had taken to each other, he did not want his protégés to feel abandoned. He sat down on the bamboo bed and asked Hujeja to make him a nice cup of unsweetened local tea.

At first, all the children were shy. Baka kept the conversation going by asking questions about their experiences of Dandimayo. He soon succeeded in engaging them in an animated discussion. There were comparisons between Banjul and Dandimayo and there was consensus that a simpler life could be interesting. Baka was fascinated by the ease with which his nieces and nephew adjusted to a different way of life. Njugga's children went out to buy some locally baked bread called Tapalapa. Massireh seized the opportunity and asked:

"Uncle Baka, why did you ask all of us to go down the hole when we were approaching Boppi Jerreh? What happened on deck? The same happened when we were about to reach Bambatenda. The only difference was we waited for a shorter period when we were in the vicinity of the latter place."

The captain was surprised by the questions. He had assumed that the story of Boppi Jerreh had been fully narrated to his nephew by his friends. He cleared his throat and began:

"Boppi Jerreh has a long history of significance to the people of Banjul and the Niumis especially fishermen and travellers down the River Gambia. It is believed that a powerful genii lives in the forefront of the island. The genii's name is Beran Sirrah. He is said to have many wives and children. There is a dangerous place in the approach to Boppi Jerreh. This is known as boom mi Beran Sirrah. Ships that dared or strayed in the vicinity of Beran Sirrah's line immediately sink. If you looked closely as we negotiated a detour, you will notice a lot of iron pointing upwards from the waters. These are all sunken boats.I understand that a very strong undercurrent sucks down any ship no matter the size. It is as strong and dangerous as the Bermuda Triangle. With time, ship and boat captains worked out a path that completely avoided boom mi Beran Sirrah.

In addition to that, it was a practice that everybody must go down the hole of the boat until the captain had singly handedly negotiated past the detour. When every passenger and sailor were down in the hole, the captain will strip off all clothes, turn his back from Boppi Jerreh and stoop in reverence to the genii. It is believed that such action would satisfy Beran Sirrah. He regarded such action as a captain's acknowledgement of his power over him. With this ritual solemnly carried out by captains, we have not heard of ship, boats and canoes capsizing in the vicinity of Boppi Jerreh.

With regards Bambatenda, it has been said that the genii was a gentle lady. She only required the captain to go through the waters alone on deck and bow in an awkward position marking deep respect for her. These were the reasons for asking all passengers to go down the hole when we were about to approach Boppi Jerreh and Bambatenda."

he boat approaching Bambatenda. Female genii in the backgrounc

Hujeja, Massireh and Ndella were silent. They could now understand why Dodou told them that he was not present to narrate what happened on deck. The captain was alone and he was the only one who knew what transpired. They had heard the story from the man himself. This was a story they would never discuss.

The return journey was uneventful. Baka's boat was full to capacity. There was no need to spend the night at Albadarr, as only a young couple alighted. The couple was replaced by two elderly women and the boat continued its journey to Banjul.

Boppi Jerreh is a small-uninhabited island. It is situated about 13 kilometres from the mouth of the River Gambia to the Atlantic Ocean. The size of this island is less than 3.5 hectares. During low tide, it is connected to the mainland of Niumi in the North Bank Region of The Gambia. The British named the place, Dog Island. Baboons are its main residents. The Wollof people of Banjul named the island Boppi Jerreh whilst the Mandingo called it Jerreh Kunjoto. The meaning of Boppi and Kunjoto is the head. The people of Banjul attached cultural importance to Boppi Jerreh, which is featured in songs at fanaal processions during the Christmas period and the celebration of Rulee Xutumba.

Chapter Two

The Birds Migrate

The sun had never been so completely hidden for days during the early part of the rainy season in the savannah belt of West Africa. Usually during this time of the year, the place was wet and humid. The weather was unbearably hot. This year was different. The weather was fabulous. Cool clean breeze blew day and night. People did not have to sleep under trees and verandahs. They didn't have to spend the whole night twisting and turning as they fanned themselves to difficult sleep with locally hand made fans. They easily slept in their houses without these hand held fans.

The first rains came in May. The ground was wet, adequate enough for the growth of early grain especially coos. The farmers were over joyed. They prepared their farms. The weeds were removed and the seeds for early coos were planted. They watched their farms nervously. After all, the rains came a bit early. There could be a long dry spell. If that happened it would be disastrous. The crops would wither and dry up. Then they would have to replant when the rains came again.

To their relief, the rains fell again a week later. All apprehension about the actual start of the rainy season slowly faded. Spirits were high among the farming community. The farmers inspected their fields and saw the young leaves of the early coos plant force themselves through the ground. Weeds of various types were growing near the crops. The farmers knew that if they allowed them they would choke their crops. They spent many long days pulling them out and setting the plants free.

The third rains came some ten days later. They showered the plants as the farmers desired. The farmers were happy for their crops that looked sturdy and healthy after the rains. They were confident that they would harvest the best crop ever. There would be plenty of grain to feed the family, to sell at 'Lumos' and therefore more money to buy other household needs.

They believed that if the rainfall pattern continued, both early and late grains would yield bumper harvests and worries of food shortages would be gone. The farmers got excited. They visited their farms daily, jealously tended and admired the plants as they developed. They were so proud that they couldn't tolerate the sight of stray grass here and there caressing the blossoming plants. Diligently, they hoed away the grass and drove strayed animals out of their fields. This was a year of great promise and expected plenty. The farmers openly and excitedly discussed their plans. They wouldn't go through the usual hungry period just before the next planting season. The assurance of enough to eat, sell and keep in food stores for a year must be secured.

This savannah area of West Africa had not experienced such pleasant weather for many decades. The environment, enveloped in luscious green was soothingly cool. The sun was never too hot. Early coos that were widely cultivated had sprouted strongly, healthily and beautifully. It was no wonder that birds started lurking around chirping musically as they flew round and round the plants. The young sons of farmers would not allow them to feast on the grains. They used their catapults to shoot at the birds in order to drive them away. These were happy and exciting moments. The young lads enjoyed their roles at the farms. It helped them improve on marksmanship.

The birds, too, were delighted. Their attempts to pick grains were not in vain. Despite all the energetic attacks of the boys, they did pick grain. They were all comfortable in the hope that there would always be more grains. They also had a second option even after the harvest.

They habitually moved further south to the forest belt of the sub-region where there was always other varieties of grains. They were contented. This mood was especially expressed in their constant singing of the song:

'Chaba chuteh, Chaba chuteh, Chuteh mbereran
Gis naneh Dougou joke nah
Douma waa jass si.'

Their melody was as sweet as that of the nightingale,
very soothing to stressed nerves. Filling the air with
their sweet song, the birds in acrobatic styles and
droves hovered over the fields all day. Theyswooped
low and then soared up to the amazement of the
farmers and their children. They were determined
that come what might; they would not be deprived
of tasting the luscious grains. Yet their amazing and
daring feats did little to gravely affect what was
perceived to be a bumper harvest. The remaining
coos stalks grew taller, sturdier and more hairy, the
grains became browner, fuller and more visible.

Worried about the obstinacy of the birds, farmers
came up with a strategy to protect the crops. Adult
farmers would work on the fields during the early
part of each day while the young boys would take
over after lunch. The birds were less troublesome
during the mornings but became very active towards
mid afternoon. The boys were challenged and in
spite of their agility they would chase the birds until
they got exhausted. The determined birds used these
periods to get down on the luscious stems and
devour some of the grains.

The remaining crops boosted the farmers'
confidence. They prayed and looked forward to a
bumper harvest. Unfortunately it was not to be. The

rains stopped. There was a long lull. The sunrays got very hot. The heat hit like a sandbag. The days became longer. It was unbearable for the farmers with hopes of an abundant harvest to watch the coos stalks tilt lifelessly to the ground as if in deference. The farmers did not give up hope. They continued to pray for rain at the beginning of each day. It did not come. Despair gradually began to creep into their hearts. Their faces became long and melancholy.

The hearty laughter and bright smiles disappeared. Sadness took over from joy, hope, confidence and expectation. The mood became infectious. The birds fell under the spell. They stopped their melodious songs. The turn of events became the daily topic of conversation with sadness and despair at its wake. They never thought of a likelihood of an extraordinary change. Therefore, they never thought of an alternative plan if the crops failed.

The dry spell continued for six weeks. The crops dried up. The water table in the area receded. The wells dried up. Farmers had to re-dig their wells. They had faith that if they could hit water there would be relief. Even where water was reached it did not last. They had to repeat the process. Soon it became obvious that it was futile to continue re-digging their wells at very short intervals.

Drinking water was in short supply. Women and children had to walk for long distances in search of both food and water. The birds suffered most. They were less resilient than the humans. They were however more realistic. They summoned a meeting outside the village of Nioro to discuss what needed to be done. One early evening, they met. The eldest bird spoke first. He opened the meeting thus:

"Mbolloh mi,
Deeklu len ma!

Just two months ago, we were a boisterous and very hopeful community. Today, we are not only very sad but also anxious. Each one of us is with a heavy heart. For this reason we gather here to decide what action we should take to survive this dire situation. This is the hardest drought we have ever experienced in this part of West Africa. During this time of the year we had always had enough to survive. Annually, at the end of the harvest of early coos, we customarily move to the forest belt with its promise of plenty. This time you are all aware the situation is different. We have to make a quick decision on what to do as a community at these extraordinary circumstances," Ngange declared.

There was silence. The elder bird had spoken. He spoke with a lot of wisdom. Then a young bird moved to the front row and requested to speak. Ngange caught sight of him and called out:

"Yes, Samba. You can add your voice."

"Mbolloh mi,
I know that I'm one of the youngest and do not have much experience to base my views. However, correct me if I'm wrong. Don't you think that since our area has become so dry we should look for other places, which offer better living conditions? We can even dare to move further north to explore those conditions. I understand there are lands where the weather conditions are different from here. White people live in those places. One of those countries has a ruler known as the queen. It is said that many people visit that country to feed pigeons. They have lots of food for birds. That's an attractive place which we should consider."

Everybody listened attentively. Most of them had never thought of going too far away from the sub-region. Others felt that they could find good conditions not too distant from their home.

The consideration was flying long distances could be tasking for the elderly. However, braver ones felt that it was better than dying of hunger. The discourse was followed by a long uncomfortable silence. Then one of the ladybirds, Linguere raised a finger to indicate that she wanted to speak. She was given the floor.

"Assalamu Alaikum, Kilifa yi ak
Mbolloh mi,

I speak on behalf of the women folk. We've listened very carefully to the previous speakers. No one here is in doubt that we must act now. We do agree with Samba's idea of moving to a land of plenty. That is migration. The issue is: which direction do we take? How do we do it? Do we all go to the same place? As it stands, we can go north now but to different places. This is the main option we have since it is premature to go south of our area to the forest belt. Some of us could cross that expansive sandy barren area known as the desert and explore countries to its north. Those who wish could live in that area known as North Africa. The younger with exceptional energy and stamina could fly for long distances and proceed to the land of the queen. I've heard that it's the land of plenty that is so attractive."

"Yes, yes, yes! Let's all go north. But we must all come back south at the opportune time. We can't miss out on the forest belt of this area."

The agreement was reached. The birds would migrate northwards for three months and then fly back to the south. They agreed to depart discreetly. They would not cause human beings to think that they were being invaded. The result could be disastrous for they could open fire on them. Thus they would move in groups of one or two families.Samba and his family headed for the land of the Queen of England. They flew day and night taking occasional breaks on their way. They kept towards the coast as they headed north. After five days of flying, they crossed a long, wide blue sea. It was the Mediterranean Sea. They were jubilant for they knew that with two more days, they would arrive late at night in the land of the Queen of England.

Birds leaving their drought stricken home

The birds were in for a surprise. The atmosphere was different. The colour of most of the people was different. The majority of them were white. There were few people who were black. Yet this did not temper their excitement. What attracted the birds most were the numerous pigeons flying around a certain area. They got curious and followed them. They reached a place where pigeons were very familiar with people.

They perched on the shoulders of white men. Other pigeons were on the ground chirping and busily eating a lot of grain thrown at them. They wondered why human beings grew their crops, harvest and then throw them on the ground as feed for pigeons. The visiting birds were even more amazed by the way in which the pigeons took their sweet time to pick the grains. Here they were not worried that young boys and men would drive them away with sticks, stones and catapults. The situation was completely different. Pigeons were loved and petted. Is this special area the much talked about Trafalgar Square? Samba wondered. No, this must be the Heaven that people in our old home talked about.

Samba was confounded by what he saw. The number of pigeons was just too much for him. He was overwhelmed by the multitude of pigeons and wondered where they came from. He got an answer. He realized that as a group from a different area they must integrate. They must mingle and study the way they behaved. Soon they succeeded. They copied and behaved just like the indigenous pigeons. This must be the means in which the numbers of pigeons had increased.

The migrant birds occasionally met and marvelled at how they survived the long journey to the land of plenty. They admitted they had no regrets for they were well fed. They were eating food through the goodwill of the people. Most of all, they enjoyed how people caressed their feathers. England had to be their abode for the next three months. They were determined to enjoy every moment.

Samba, because of his youth and friendliness gained many friends. He took care of himself. He bathed very early every morning; smooth his plumes and paraded himself with a lot of confidence. He caught the attention of many bird loving people. Not even the pigeons that had been there for a long time regarded him as a stranger. He had attractive mannerisms that were imitated by many. He discreetly competed for attention and was determined to outdo birds that have been in England longer. He succeeded. He and his friends had a good and memorable time. Yet they knew that because of the distance they had to cover to get to England, they must leave early to reach their destination as scheduled. They must reach the forest belt of West Africa in good time in accordance with tradition for the latter part of the year.

Linguere and her friends, the other group of birds that were not so adventurous did not go too far away from their abode. Their keen sense of smell of human beings led them to a nearby kingdom known as Jolof. It was ruled by a very young, admirable and adorable king. He had four wives and other consensual partners. Linguere and her friends were lured by the smell of ripening findi crop to the fields of Burr Njai's subjects. They settled down in the nearby bush for the night. They had an enjoyable dinner from the findi. They decided to pay their respects to the king at his palace on the next day. That night they planned the manner in which they would present themselves to the king as they were seven in number. They would transform themselves into three gentlemen and four ladies. Linguere, who had admirable leadership qualities and a sophisticated manner, would be the best dressed. She must attract the king through her well-mannered and feminine demeanour. The others would pose as married couples. If the king were successfully attracted, Linguere would undoubtedly be invited to stay and perhaps work in the royal household.

The next morning, Linguere assisted by her companions went to the Lumo to buy appropriate clothing. The visit was scheduled for late afternoon when the king would have taken a break with his Council of Elders. They went and at the main palace gate, in a very dignified manner, the group explained to the guards thus:

"We have just migrated to this beautiful and peaceful kingdom. Tradition demands that as strangers we should come to the king to announce our presence. This is not only a mark of respect but an obligation due to every ruler particularly this admirable one. We must adhere to the obligation. Thus we are here to make a courtesy call on His Royal Highness the king."

The group's introductory remarks were so impressive that the guards had no option but to oblige. One of the guards treated them as very important people. He led them to a big luxurious and tastefully furnished chamber with strong kenno wooden armchairs, couches and a handsomely finished golden throne. The king was sitting on the throne chatting amicably with a group of elderly men. They were laughing heartily when the visitors entered. After the curtsying and bowing for the king and his Council of Elders, the guests were invited to sit down. Linguere was the spokesperson. She spoke thus:

"Your Royal Highness
 Distinguished elders
We are here to formally announce our presence in the kingdom. We wish to settle here and become subjects of Your Royal Highness, Burr Njai. Thus we come to pay our respects to you, your Council of Elders and your entire household. We are hopeful to receive your formal approval to stay here. In adhering to tradition we humbly announce our presence and pledge allegiance to you, the admirable and benevolent ruler.

Burr, the progress and prosperity of this kingdom are known far and wide. Your subjects have spoken about your good leadership and your particular consideration for their welfare. It is no wonder that they are really proud of you. People in other kingdoms in our sub-region hope to reach the heights you have taken your people. For us, we want to live on hope. We want to be part of success. Thus we are here because of our desire not only to benefit from your natural kindness but also to participate in the development of this kingdom. We are therefore at your service. Allow me, Your Royal Highness to formally introduce members of our group.

The gentleman with the short, scanty beard is Njugga. He's a skilled and experienced carpenter. Sitting next to Njugga is his wife, Majiguene. She is a seamstress who is very creative in original designs. The clean-shaven man is a professional painter. His name is Badara. He prefers a clean head because of his baldness. He was regarded as the best painter in our old community. Sitting right next to him is his wife, Kumba. Kumba is both a hairdresser and a beautician. She personally did the njam on her lower and upper gums and her chin. This was an indication of the high level of skill she had acquired in her profession. Sitting here on my immediate left is Ndeye. She is a rice farmer and vegetable gardener. During her leisure time she is a fortuneteller. She was the one who predicted that we would one day become the subjects of a prosperous and generous king. Our presence here today has proven her right. Her husband, Falley is the one on my immediate right. Sirs, don't be deceived by his small eyes, which seem closed. He's wide-awake. We joke that he concentrates too much when he is plastering the walls of houses. He's a good mason. I'm sure that he would be very useful in the kingdom.

Lastly, let me introduce myself. I am Linguere. I've been called to many weddings and naming ceremonies to head the cooking team. Our people said that I cook tasteful Cheebu jen no matter how important the occasion and how large the crowd. These are the skills we are endowed with as a group. We are wholeheartedly at your disposal," concluded Linguere.

The king and his council members looked at each other. They then turned their eyes to the guests. Burr Njai could not remember how long ago he had seen a skilled group of people settle in the kingdom. He was impressed. He spoke:

"Council Elders and Dear guests
I'm amazed at the diversity of such a group. Your skills reassure us that you've not come here only to benefit from our goodwill but also to offer your contributions to the development of our nation. Therefore, I welcome you all here. Feel at home. You'll indeed find work in this place where the people are very hardworking and skillful. Since you've just come, my able Head of Administration, Jimba Saye will find placement in the community for each of you. I'm sure that council elders will welcome another well-trained cook in the palace. Linguere, where did you get your name? My sister's name is Linguere. " Burr Njai shot a quick smile at Linguere.

Linguere looked at her friends and then said:

"I don't know the history of my name. But I'm an only child to my mother and father. May be that's the reason. They both treated me as their princess.

Thank you very much, Burr for readily giving me the opportunity to serve you as a cook in this magnificent palace. I'll do my best to give you the best. Your Royal Highness, members of the Council of Elders, I am at your service."

"Jimba, you can take care of them. Introduce Linguere to the members of the royal family and the rest of the household," the king directed.

With such instructions, Jimba led the visitors out of the room after the final courtesies. Linguere stole a look at the king and their eyes met and held. The message was attraction, Linguere mused as she moved away. Jimba told the visitors to return to the palace the next morning. By that time, all the necessary arrangements as instructed by the king would have been worked out.

The group returned to their home satisfied with the outcome of the visit. They immediately began to lay their plans of operation. They must integrate into the community. However, they should never betray their original beings. They must behave and conduct themselves as human beings for the next few months. Linguere was warned to be particularly careful. The fact that she had secured a job at the palace on the first visit could cause jealousy in people. She must be very diplomatic in her interactions. She must endear herself to every member of the royal household and confided these intentions of winning the hearts of all members of the royal family to her companions. With regards the king, she would work hard on that message from their first eye contact to achieve a fully-fledged attraction. That way she would gain more.

Linguere was mindful that this could bring about jealousy among other royal workers. The other cooks would closely monitor her. She would therefore behave discreetly and most importantly keep her identity secret. They all agreed that at the end of each day, they would bring grain home for their dinner.

The others, who were not as lucky as Linguere, were committed to working hard. They took up the responsibility to bring home any quantity of uncooked grain they could get. They realized that eating cooked food could create health problems for them. They agreed to avoid eating that type of food but in a manner that would be unnoticed. When invited they would pretend to eat. They would eat from the same food bowl with the people. However, they would cleverly and carefully push the food away from their side of the bowl towards the other people in the process of eating. The important thing was to ensure that their fingers had some of the food. Hence they would seem to be eating but they would not swallow the food. As birds they were not used to go for long hours without food. It would be a challenge they must face. Yet they would have to resist the urge to take some uncooked grain to nibble. They must cultivate discipline.

They arrived at the palace the next day. Jimba had made all arrangements. The visitors were taken to work at different places according to their trades. Linguere joined the team responsible for the food of the royal family. The Head Cook, Aram with an endearing smile addressed Linguere:

"Come, young lady, tell us about yourself. What dishes can you cook very well? Here we have a duty roster and each of us cook what she does best."

Linguere explained respectfully:

"My name is Linguere. I came from Yoon Wi. Our country was struck by drought. All our crops died. That's why we left in search of work and a better standard of living. Apart from cooking for my family, I used to lead the group of special female cooks who prepare food for marriages, naming ceremonies and other important occasions. Our people praised us for producing delectable dishes namely: Cheebu jen, Maafeh, and Soupa Kandia."

"Good! Then you'll have to come in the mornings. These dishes are eaten as midday meals. You'll therefore work every day. When you're not cooking, you'll help with other kitchen chores. Your day would end after cleaning the utensils. This would be around early evening. Since this is your first day, you'll not cook. You'll only observe how we operate," directed Aram. She turned to leave but then stopped. She addressed Linguere in a softer tone:

"We've heard a lot about the drought that hit your area. It's really a pity that you people worked so hard only to lose your crops. Thank God you've the good sense to relocate. I wish it didn't have to happen. But then we can't turn back the hands of time. You're with your own here. Feel comfortable." Aram took Linguere's hand and gently squeezed it. Linguere flashed a grateful smile. Aram left the room. Linguere went to the kitchen.

The new cook worked very hard that day and did whatever she was told by her senior colleagues. During lunch she pretended to eat withthem although she did not swallow any cooked food. In the evening when she was about to go home, Aram gave her a good handful of coos because she stayed a bit longer to help with the preparation of dinner. She was too happy to receive the small tip.

Linguere returned home to find her companions had already arrived. They had all transformed to their natural beings: birds. They flapped their wings and danced around when they saw what Linguere had brought along. They could not compare it with what they had brought along for dinner: good old coos, as they knew it. First day over, they retired in order to start early on the next day.

The women working in the palace kitchen welcomed Linguere's willingness. She did the menial chores they disliked: pounding pepper and onions, cleaning the big cooking pots, dishes and other kitchen utensils. She readily offered to serve the king whenever a waiter was absent. Gradually, she worked her way into the hearts of the people she served. She was the soft-spoken waitress and the clean and neat cook who put tasty food on the table. The king spoke of his wise decision in making her join the royal staff. Linguere endeared herself to the king's sister and the eldest princess, Linguere. The princess called the young cook, namesake.

Linguere maintained a cordial relationship with everyone in the palace. Whenever it was her turn to cook, Burr Njai invited members of the Council of Elders to stay for lunch. Everyone looked forward to her food. She cooked delicious dishes and served them attractively and with pleasant words and smiles. She wisely kept her recipes secret. No one saw how she improved on the taste of the food. The king, his sisters and the queens spoke of Linguere's tasty food.

Aram grew to like Linguere. Whenever she had duties away from the palace, she would entrust Linguere with the keys of the food store of the palace. By the time she was two months at the job, Linguere had access to everything. The other cooks became jealous. One day, as the group was gossiping, a senior cook Maram said:

"Hey, have you noticed? Aren't you amazed at how Linguere has become so important? I can't believe that Linguere who came not long ago has got everybody liking her. Everyone ask her to do errands.

She's been given more responsibilities than any of us, we, the old hands. This is not natural. To add salt into injury, Aram sometimes gives her the much-coveted keys to the food store of this palace. Imagine! Even Burr Njai talks about her good and delicious food. He only invites people to lunch when she cooks. The king's eldest sister calls Linguere her namesake. The queens dote on her. What is this? Has she staged a palace coup? If she hasn't, she's well on her way to it. We have to be very careful. Otherwise she'll uproot us. Do you remember that she moved here with three other women? She must be planning to get us replaced by them. Let's not underestimate her. She's very smart."

Another cook named Metta chipped in:

"You're very observant, Maram. Linguere is a sly and tricky lady. If you tell her to put her finger in the hot cooking stove, she'll do it without getting burnt. She's that tricky. We've got to be very watchful. Otherwise she'll soon become our boss and then kick us out of here. She's already the favourite of the important members of the royal family."

"I agree with Metta that this stranger should be watched. We have to fault her. Otherwise she'll succeed in not only overshadowing us but also replacing the whole kitchen with her own people," Maram commented.

"We'll watch her every move. Let's not only criticize what she does but also come up with innovative ideas as suggestions. That way, we can disguise our motive of discrediting her," added Metta.

They chorused their agreement to launch an immediate campaign to discredit Linguere. She had been in the palace for a shorter period of time than all of them. Yet she had become a very powerful employee. This development must quickly be stopped. As soon as they closed the discussion, Linguere walked in. Her keen ears had picked the mention of her name and Metta's last sentence. She did not show them she heard part of what was said. Linguere had just finished serving lunch to Burr Njai in his private chambers. The king had romantically hugged her, touched her firm breasts and caressed her nipples. The startling feelings that invaded her body were like electrical shocks. She did not resist the king's advances. Her body wanted more but she was too shy to reciprocate. She was well aware that the king had four wives and three taaras. They all lived comfortably in different chambers within the palace. She knew she could never become a queen. A romantic relationship with the king would have to be a well-guarded secret. When Linguere did not openly react to his moves, the king let her go. He knew there would be another opportunity to sweep her off her feet.

Before leaving the king's room, Linguere adjusted herself. She took the dirty dishes and hurriedly left. She was overwhelmed by the new feelings. She paid little attention to what she overheard as she entered the kitchen until later. In her daze she muttered inaudible greetings to her colleagues as she placed the dirty dishes near the well. She then sent a glance at the kitchen to see whether there were other dirty utensils. There were none. The place looked glitteringly clean so she completed her chore. Her colleagues tauntingly said that they had cleaned everything whilst she was busy serving the king. She was upset. She became quiet and very pensive. Maram noticed. She was anxious with the fear that Linguere had overheard them when they were laying out their wicked plan. With hidden guilt she asked:

"Linguere, you've been behaving strangely since you stepped your foot in the kitchen. Why are you so quiet? Is anything wrong? Are you tired? I can help you with whatever you have to do. Go and take a rest. We must have been overworking you."

"Oh no, Maram! I like doing my work. I'd finish cleaning these dishes and then go home early. I'm a bit exhausted. That's all," replied Linguere.

"You can leave the rest of the dishes. I'll do them. Now, be a good girl and go home. Get a good rest. You'll feel fresh in the morning," coaxed Maram.

Linguere allowed Maram to have her way. She left the three remaining dishes and went to the changing room to get ready. She had some uncooked coos in the bag as well as her clean clothes. She took a quick bath, got dressed and left for home. When she was out of sight, Metta said:

"We've not even started our campaign and she's getting exhausted. It's always good to take on what is manageable. Our young lady is trying to be a super woman. Perhaps we don't need a campaign to derail her after all. We can get her tired by heaping most of our work on her. Since she's willing, she won't complain. She'll make many mistakes which would bring her down."

"We can use both your strategy and mine. The sooner she fails, the better," replied Maram. "The two of us would tidy up the cooking area and then leave for home."

Linguere on the other hand was in deep thought on her way home. She was still in her human form of a young woman. She was savouring the electrical but sweet feeling that she experienced when the king made the amorous moves. Burr Njai's touch introduced her to a new type of feeling she had never known before. She did enjoy it. This inexplicably wonderful feeling only known by humans must be why men and women get married. The feeling is very powerful, more powerful than lightning. We, birds do not have anything like this type of sensation. Perhaps that's why we mate and move on. No strings attached. Linguere tried to understand the emotion she felt from the king's touch whilst she was in his room.

Linguere, still in a daze walked and reached home without realizing it. It was when she heard the exciting noises of her companions that she came to her senses. She hurriedly shifted her shape to her original form of a bird. She went through her usual evening routine of emptying her working bag of the uncooked coos. Her companions had already put down what they had. They gathered round the heap of grain to dine. As they slowly nibble their food, they took turns to narrate the highlights of their day.

Linguere dreaded for her turn to come. She did not dare to narrate what happened in Burr Njai's room. Then she remembered what she overheard as she approached the kitchen. That would be a suitable story for her to tell. She did. She told her friends that the women in the kitchen were getting jealous of her. She had heard them talking about her as she approached the kitchen. She was not too sure what sort of plot they had hatched for her. She however suspected that they wanted to see her downfall. Her peers offered their advice to her. They were confident that if the king and his sisters knew what the others had planned, they would protect her. The royal family should be told. Linguere did not want to do such a thing because she would have no control over the consequences. She decided to tread cautiously and avoid angering the senior kitchen staff.

Linguere had a sleepless night. She was torn between her strong feelings for Burr Njai and the fear of discovery of what had happened between them. She pondered deeply about how far her colleagues at the palace would go to destroy her. Later, she drifted to a light sleep but woke up thrice during the night.

The next morning, Linguere asked Kumba, the hairdresser who had a free day to take a message for her to Aram at the palace. She should inform her that she was unwell. Kumba should offer Aram to take over Linguere's duties. Kumba did. Aram needed the help and therefore accepted. She displayed concern about Linguere's health but Kumba assured her that she should recover by the next day.

The other cooks were suspicious when they saw Kumba. They were fearful that Linguere had succeeded in facilitating the recruitment of her friend into the palace. Maram, who was the brazen one among them, questioned Kumba:

"Hey! Who are you? Where's Linguere? Has she left the job? What is she doing today? We've not seen her yet. Is she gone to see the king or her namesake?"

Kumba coolly replied:

"Linguere is at home. She's not feeling well. She asked me to come and inform Aram that she can't come to work today. I'm Kumba, Linguere's friend. I'm a hairdresser."

"Oh! We're so sorry to hear that she wasn't feeling well. We must go and see her when we're off duty. She's such a willing girl. Perhaps, we'll go and see her tomorrow." Relieved Maram spoke for the rest. Kumba noticed and didn't like the way they exchanged glances. She walked away.

By midday, the whole palace had heard that the new cook was ill. The king's sister, older Linguere summoned Aram and Kumba to her chambers.She wanted to hear about the nature of Linguere's illness. As soon as they entered her room, she addressed Aram:

"I heard this morning that my namesake is unwell. What's wrong with her? Is it serious? We must call in the local doctor if she continues to be unwell. She's a hardworking and willing young woman."

"Your Highness, let me introduce you to the person who she sent to me. This is Kumba. She's a hairdresser. Linguere asked her to tell me she was ill.

She has stayed on to help me with Linguere's duties. She's here. Your Highness, she'll tell you what's wrong with your namesake," Aram replied nodding at Kumba to go ahead and explain. Kumba then explained:

"Your Highness, Linguere had a bad night. She couldn't sleep and woke up feeling dizzy. She tried to force herself to come to work but she fell down when she came out of the bathroom. She had asked me to come to the palace to get her to be excused from duty by Aram. I am also to hold the fort for my friend. I'm sure that after a good day's rest Linguere will be back at work tomorrow."

The king's sister, Elder Linguere seemed relieved. She addressed Kumba thus:

"So, you are the creative hairdresser and beautician who came to settle here with Linguere! I hope you're very busy. The women of this kingdom take good care of themselves. They are very particular about their looks. One of these days I'll ask Linguere to bring you along so that you can plait my hair beautifully and apply fudan on my nails."

"I'll come any time you wish, Your Royal Highness. I'll do you a unique hairstyle that has never been worn in our generation.Even the patterns of the fudan on your nails will be unique. I am at your service, Your Highness," Kumba graciously replied curtsying for the Elder Linguere.

Aram was mesmerized by the hairdresser's grace. She had to gently pull Kumba out of the room with her in order to return to the work place. Aram though was not jealous of Kumba. She found her just as willing and helpful as Linguere. She ran errands and made sure that the kitchen was clean for those coming in the early evening shift to cook dinner. She was so pleased with Kumba that she gave her presents of uncooked coos and rice to take home. Aram was unaware how much these small presents of uncooked grain meant to Linguere and Kumba.

Linguere was well enough to go to work the next day. Everyone in the palace showed concern over her health. Aram put her on light duty. Nevertheless, she closed work in the early evening as was usual.

Kumba has always been known for her sharp ears. On this particular evening on her way home, she thought she heard birds singing. She listened attentively. The song grew louder. The tune sounded familiar. As the singing continued, she realized that it was their rallying song. Could this be a sign that some of the birds were returning to their home in the savannah belt? With the constant repetition of the melody, she was convinced that the time had come for them to return home. Involuntarily, her body began to react to the music. She was transforming. First her head then the limbs followed and finally the whole body became that of a bird.

'Chaba chuteh, Chaba chuteh,

Automatically, she joined in the singing of the song:
Chuteh mbereran
Dougoub nyorr na
Chouti mbereran
Chaba chouti Chaba chuteh
Chouti mbereran
Nyibi jotna chouti mbereran
Nyi jotna chouti mbereran
Chouti chabah chout yerereh
Chouti chabah, Chout yerrereh
Chouti chabah, Chout yerrereh.'

Singing the song Kumba flew home to Linguere and
her other companions. The song said everything. It
was the rallying call. Time was up for them to move
to the forest belt. They all had mixed feelings. They
had really liked their lives as human beings. Most of
all they enjoyed their varied experiences. They had
the best of two worlds at the same time: human and
bird. They must now prepare to go back to their
natural origins. They must say goodbye to the people
of Jolof.

This was a thought that they had always pushed away
from their minds. They must now face it squarely.
They were at a loss. They did not know how to say
goodbye. The people had treated them as their own
kin. Thus Linguere and her friends spent the best
part of the night planning their exit. They planned to
withdraw one at a time to avoid being noticed.
Those who were not engaged in any prominent work
would be the first to leave. Ndeye, Njugga,

Magiguene, Badara and Falley would leave immediately. Kumba and Linguere could not be early leavers. They would have to wait. After doing the hair and nails of the king's eldest sister, it would be appropriate for Kumba to leave. Linguere would follow at a later time.

Linguere returned to work the next day confused and feeling deeply depressed. It was her turn to cook. She had to conceal the great internal conflict within her. She would cook her best meal and serve the king with his lunch. She succeeded in controlling her nervousness whilst the king ate. He praised her cooking skills and remarked favourably about the delicious food he was having for lunch. He was indeed in a good mood. Linguere was pleased with the praises but deep down she was in turmoil. She knew that her days in Jolof were numbered.

When Burr Njai finished eating, Linguere rose in order to clear the dishes. He gently pulled her to himself, placed her on his lap. He brushed her lips with a long passionate kiss. Linguere weakly tried to disengage herself. She actually did not want to move away from him. She was torn between her burning desire for the king and common sense. The desire was stronger. She followed her heart and stayed a bit longer. By the time she left the king's chambers, she was more confused than ever. She knew that their relationship was going to be short lived.

She told herself that she must leave as soon as possible before people suspected them. Any gossip about their relationship would jeopardise her position in the palace. The queens and taaras would turn against her. She couldn't predict the reaction of the king's sister, her namesake. She knew that her co-workers who had hatched a plan of discrediting her would have a field day. She would be isolated and become a laughing stock. The longer she stayed, the more difficult it would become to get away. Therefore, she had to and must immediately leave. The nights were filled with singing of the rallying song.

Two days after the warm encounter, the king's sister, Elder Linguere asked for Kumba to come over to the palace. A grand ndow rabin was to be held in the kingdom. The women were getting ready for this celebration. Elder Linguere wanted Kumba to plait her hair in the promised unique style. She would also apply henna on her nails, palms and feet with intricate patterns. True to her promise, Kumba did the princess's hair in a style never seen before in the kingdom. The designs of the henna on her nails were so artistic that the best beautician would never be able to reproduce them. The princess was very happy. She gave Kumba a present, which was one of her nicely made cotton clothes. She promised to retain her as her only hairdresser and beautician.

Unfortunately, that was never to be. Kumba had planned to leave that very night. Linguere helped

Kumba to prepare for her departure. They transformed themselves to their original forms to the accompaniment of the rallying song. Linguere was depressed and home sick. She would be alone when Kumba left. She couldn't overcome her mood even though she tried to be light-hearted by joining in the song:

'Chaba chouteh, Chaba chouteh, Chouteh mbereran
Suma yeek gone neh Dougoub nior naa
Choute mbereran
Dou ma saye ak Bai Burr Njai
Chouti mbereran
Dou ma saye ak Baye Burr Njai
Chouti mberaran
Chouteh chabah, Chu yerrereh
Chu chabah, Chu yerrereh.

Linguere continued singing the rallying song until Kumba spread out her wings, spunned round, hugged and pecked Linguere on the beak before she slowly and surely flew higher and higher towards the direction of the music. She found it difficult to leave Linguere behind but had to muster courage and flew away. Linguere perched on a high tree and watched her friend as she flew until she disappeared. I'll soon go the same way, she muttered to herself as she went back to her already deserted abode.

Linguere went to bed. All her companions had left. However, she looked forward to the time of the day that she spent in the palace. She was comfortable in the fact that the royal family and the people of Jolof did not notice the absence of Linguere's companions. Most of them did not have much to do and were not seen often. Thus the people of Jolof did not miss Linguere's group. They were believed to be engaged in other activities.

Linguere stayed on for a while. During that time, she quietly prepared for her departure while she continued serving the royal family just as before. Mentally, she had reconciled her emotions with the fact that she was a bird. Thus she had nothing to lose in leaving the infatuated relationship with the king behind. She was at work up to the last night before her departure. She enjoyed the attentions of Burr Njai and was adept in the way she concealed her intentions. At the close of work for that day, she did receive a bit of grain from Aram which she did not need as she was going to have a lone dinner. She planned to leave that night.

On the way home, Linguere heard the usual rally song in the distance. This was the final call for her to go and join her kind. She went and found her companions had assembled. They were waiting for her to fly south to the forest belt. Her spirits lifted as she remembered the good times they had had in the forest area in the past. She was happy she wouldn't miss this year. The song was repeated again and again. In spite of herself she chorused loudly:

'Chaba chouteh, Chaba chouteh, Chouteh mbereran

Suma yaek gone neh Dougoub nior naa
Chute mbereran
Dou ma saye ak Bai Burr Njai
Chouteh mbereran
Dou ma saye ak Baye Burr Njai
Chouteh mbereran
Chouteh chabah, Chu yerrereh
Chu chabah, Chu yerrereh.

With the singing of the song, her shape began to
shift. Her head became that of a bird. Then the rest
of her body changed completely. She looked around
what she was about to abandon and a cry escaped
from her. She rose and slowly lifted herself up with a
flutter. She flew away following the direction from
which the song was coming. She was going to join
the rest of her clan. The time was opportune for
them to move south to the forest belt. They must go
at once.

Linguere found all the birds gathered at the
designated place. Those who went to Trafalgar
Square in London arrived a few days before her. As
they waited for late night, they exchanged stories
about their experiences during their tour. In the
middle of the night when all human beings were
deep in sleep, the birds left for their journey in
search of more ripe grain in the forest belt of West
Africa.

Chapter Three

Kumba Ndaba marries Jeggan Touray

Kumba Ndaba lived in the village of Nayak. This was a village with many trees although it was not located in the thick forest belt. There were big Santang, mango, orange and baobab trees. The village was green, grassy and leafy. One could walk around the whole village without trampling on the bare sand. Even during the rainy season when temperatures were high, Nayak's weather was different. One could go jogging for a distance without breaking a sweat. The village was that cool. It was heaven on earth. This was bee land. The bees considered themselves blessed to live in such a congenial environment.

The village was a special place. It was blessed. Its inhabitants were young, energetic with a good number of beautiful females that could not be found in the neighbouring localities. One of those beauties was called Kumba Ndaba. She had a beautiful body, long and moderately covered. Her abdomen, though well spread, was hardly noticeable. Her arms and legs had firm well-shaped muscles just like an athlete. For a bee, she had a shapely figure well toned because of her passion of maintaining a healthy, sportive body. Her rounded jaws, when opened, displayed very sharp teeth. Kumba was certainly a queen bee. Her curved, smooth stinger was an added asset. She could repeatedly use it without endangering her own life. Her beauty was such that heads involuntarily turned when she walked past. Her confidence added to her attractiveness.

Jeggan Touray was destined to fall in love with the beauty of Nayak and later betrothed to her. He lived in a big Santang tree not far from Kumba Ndaba's family home. The eldest and only son of Ndeye and Samba Touray, Jeggan was a thoughtful and respectable son. He was by his parents' side during the collection of food for the family. Food was therefore never scarce in their home. Neighbours talked about how fortunate the Touray family was to have such a dutiful son.

Kumba's parents, Mbissin and Baye Ndongo knew the Touray family. They had cordial but not very close neighbourly relations. One day, Jeggan and his father went out to look for food and met up Baye Ndongo.

"Hello, Baye. How are you?" Samba warmly greeted him.

"Oh! Is that you, Samba? I'm fine. I'm just out to gather food for Mbissin and my daughter, Kumba. Who do you have with you today?" Baye Ndongo enquired.

"Ah! I've got my son, Jeggan with me." Turning to Jeggan he said:

"You've not met Uncle Baye? Son, this is Uncle Baye. He lives with his family at the Santang tree not far from us. He's the proud father of the beauty of Nayak."

"Hey, that's another marvelous act. We're grateful for the offer. Thank you so much, dear Samba. Jeggan, here is an open invitation. Come again to see us. You don't have to wait for your father to come with you here. You're our son and as such always welcomed to our home," Baye stated. The gifts of food were graciously accepted. Baye could not measure how much the acceptance and words meant to Samba.

Samba and his son moved in silence back home. They kept their separate thoughts to themselves. They did not confer. Samba with the feeling of exaltation could not keep it all to himself. When he was alone with his wife, Ndeye he narrated what happened at Baye's compound. This visit sowed the seed of speculation. Dreams of a union of their son, the most eligible bachelor to the most beautiful girl in the area was constantly in their mouths. They looked forward to a repeat visit when Samba would register Jeggan's interest in Kumba. They anticipated that before a second visit, Samba and his wife would confer with their son to find out whether he was interested in the damsel.

Three days after the eventful visit to Baye's home, Samba and Ndeye casually talked admiringly about

Kumba whilst they were eating with Jeggan. Samba itched to test the waters on Jeggan's feelings. He started the conversation thus:

"Jeggan, what do you think about Kumba Ndaba? I'm sure you're dying for us to talk about her."

Jegaan stared at them with a little surprise. He was suspicious that his parents would bring up the subject. He however, never thought that it would come so soon.

"Well, she'...a beauty. She could... be fun to be with. Although I like her, I don't... know her very well. Why...are you asking?" Jeggan stammered bashfully. Samba, not very confidently this time went on:

"You see, your mother and I have talked a lot about our last visit to Baye's home. We're both convinced that they like us. They would be too happy to be honoured with a proposal of betrothal between you and their daughter. Of course this is not now but later. You're still young and need a bit more time to know each other. For now, we will be happy with the simple formal expression of interest in Kumba on your behalf. What do you think about that?" Samba asked.

"I'll do anything that would make you and my mother happy,"replied the still baffled Jeggan.

What else could he say? They are his beloved parents but more importantly he liked Kumba Ndaba very much and as far as he could sense, she seemed to respond to the same feelings. Elated and satisfied on the expressed feeling of each member of the family, the issue was signed and sealed.

Samba and Ndeye heeded the old wife's saying: acts that are rushed end in disaster. They decided to move at a reasonable pace. The next step, an informal talk with Kumba Ndaba's parents should be done not exuberantly but with dignity. Jeggan's parents held on the need to delay a bit, on the hope of the desirable development.

Destiny would not allow things to happen as planned. Baye and Mbissin, in spite of their belief, had the urge to return Samba's visit. Their daughter, Kumba, secretly excitedly, begged to accompany them two weeks later. Samba's family was pleasantly surprised. The welcome was exciting. They did not expect a visit so soon from Baye and his family. The exchange of visits went further to cement this flowering relationship between the two families. The civil exchanges were very cordial generating a comfortable atmosphere for some adult conversation. Samba descreetly attentive to the demeanour of Kumba and Jeggan jokingly said at one point:

"Hum, the young ones are showing that they are not being left behind. They're talking to each other and their conversation seems engaging. They are not aware of us. Have you noticed? They're in their own world."

"We, their parents are friends. It is natural that they too become friends. They should cherish having each other. This is how families become so close that they become relatives. And who knows. This can develop further than we imagine," replied Baye.

The two sets of parents clearly indicated to their children that they were appreciative of more than a cordial relationship. The youths understood what was being demonstrated.

The signals were loud and clear. The youngsters had the ball in their court. The strengthening of the relationship rested squarely on their shoulders. The onus was on them to respect the wishes of parents.

Time did not stand still. A month after the significant visit, Samba thought it fitting to take some honeycombs to his friend, Baye. This, he figured out would be seen as a symbolic demonstration of Jeggan's interest in Kumba.

Baye Ndongo and his wife graciously accepted the gifts. With a deep sigh of relief, they felt they were close to getting the most eligible and respectable son for their daughter. The largest delectable piece of honeycomb was ostentatiously placed on the door to Kumba's room. This meant that no other suitor could come to her. She was committed. The gift of that special honeycomb put the relationship between the two families to an endearing level. A bond became a reality. The parents maintained a keen interest in the development of the relationship between Kumba and Jeggan. Their objective of marriage between the two must be realised.

Kumba and Jeggan grew closer. Timidity was gradually loosening its grip. Jeggan made casual visits to Kumba's home. Exchanges of niceties gave way to simple jokes. They became comfortable in each other's company. This was what their parents had secretly hoped for. They were close and had come to like each other. There would be no need to nudge the youngsters to marriage. They would take the initiative themselves. It would be a natural sequence to the strong emotional feeling displayed by Jeggan to Kumba. The time came sooner than the parents expected. Jeggan approached his parents and confidently said:

"You know, Papa I'm at a loss as to how to tell you this. Lately I've kept thinking of that day when you told me that you wanted Kumba Ndaba to be my future wife. At the time, I was taken aback for I wasn't sure of my emotions. However, today, I think differently. You as the good parents you've always been to me had a wish and told me. Your dear wish must be a directive to be adhered to. I believe it is my duty to oblige. I can safely say that I know and love Kumba Ndaba well enough to want her as my wife. I have discussed marriage with her. We are both committed to spending our lives together. I am certain this news is comforting to you. I want you to meet her family so that negotiations for an appropriate wedding would commence. Papa, Papa, pray for us. This union must be for a lifetime. It should uplift both families."

Samba hid a smile. He shot a quick furtive look at his wife. A powerful sensation whether of excitement or excessive joy seized Samba. The emotions took charge of his powers of speech and thinking. He was mute and his meaningless gaze was fixed to empty space. His wife, Ndeye, overwhelmed by the reaction of her husband, shouted: 'Samba, Samba, 'ya ngeh chalit' at the top of her voice. Rigorous shaking of the shoulders jolted Samba back to awareness. With Ndeye by his side massaging the face, around the eyes, the cheeks right down the chin, the functions of each gradually became restored. A huge yawn said everything. Samba 'came back'. Minutes slipped by before Samba uttered these sentences:

"My son, we've been waiting for this day for some time. Your mother and I denied ourselves sleep for months. We devoted the nights to prayers for our fervent wish of securing the hand of the most eligible maiden of the land in marriage for our dearest son.

Your declaration of intent is an indication of the Almighty's gracious answer to our prayers. Let me assure you, my beloved son that time would not be wasted. The processes governing the traditional rites and rituals would be set in motion immediately."

The preliminary step of declaring the intention of seeking Kumba Ndaba in marriage was taken the next Friday by Jeggan's parents to the head of Baye Ndongo's family. It was a meeting of equals. Great warmth and extraordinary faith was the atmosphere through which the talks were held. Each party jealously guarded its position in society. It was, therefore, no surprise that the bride's parents displayed considerable goodwill in naming the amount for the bride price. The beauty of the maiden, her high eligibility did not influence the parents. The consideration was compliance with tradition. This was marvelous restraint being expressed. It was gracious.

Samba's delegation was left mesmerized. The big question they had to answer was: 'how such magnanimity could be reciprocated?' Already they had overspent their ideas during the euphoria, which followed Jeggan's declaration of love for Kumba. They had taken the biggest honeycomb in the land as gift for the first visit. The gift was well received. Friends, relatives and neighbours licked their lips and fingers on touch and taste of a piece. Now, the bride's family had left the issue of an exclusive gift to them. This was a real challenge. Time was short.

The main bridal gift to be taken prior to the wedding date had yet to be obtained. The head of delegation was in despair. He could not think. Desperately, he cried out:

"Why, oh why is my mind failing me to identify an appropriate present? Weak mind, must you make me a failure to Samba? If so, why do I have you inside me? Weak mind, strengthen up and show me a fitting present soonest."

Divine intervention came to his aid. An idea visited. The delegation agreed that the first present that was so well received should be multiplied. The quantities that they should present should fill the largest store in the neighbourhood. The quality should be premium. Nobody should have tasted such quality of honeycombs.

The head of delegation went aside and shared his thoughts with his group. They agreed that his idea, though challenging, was the best. They went back to the bride's delegation and informed them that they would come up with an impressive bride's gift.

Preparations for the big day immediately commenced. Kumba's mother and aunts were happy to a feverish pitch. According to tradition, it was their role to feed and entertain the guests. Kumba was the most eligible maiden on the land in beauty and demeanour. Expectations in the community were high and attendance at the celebrations would be numerous. Kumba's mother, Mbissin was determined that food had to be plenty. Collection of different types of honeycombs was obligatory. Space for storage must be available. The male members of the family built a big store.

Two days to the wedding, Samba gave notice to the bride's family that the bridal gift would be delivered the next day. Speculations were rife within the bride's family. What constituted the gift for the bride? It was a puzzle. Let's wait and see.

At the agreed day, Samba's delegation appeared. They were 'loaded'. Baye Ndongo's family received them. They were perplexed. The greetings were short. Delivery of the present started. Honeycombs nicely wrapped, were delivered in lots and lots. Many hands came to assist. Display and storage had to be carefully done. The process seemed unending. Kumba's family was overwhelmed. Gracious friends and neighbours were at hand to help. The huge stores carefully prepared were full to capacity. Nothing short of wonderment reigned the whole evening. Samba's delegation deeply satisfied, courteously begged to leave after the presentation of the gifts.

The solemn and dignified wedding ceremony took place at Kumba Ndaba's home. All the inhabitants of Nayak and its environs attended it. The eldest male bee led the ceremony. He called the names of the couple and prayed for them. This sanctified the union of Kumba Ndaba and Jeggan Touray.

Bees especially from the elite class celebrated their weddings in style. Kumba and Jeggan's union was wedding of the century. The reception was the first of its kind. The honeycombs that came from different flowers were succulent. They were served continuously. The merriment was in various forms, catering for entertainment for every age. It went on to the early hours of the morning.

Guests from different distant places left but many stayed particularly members of both families. The bride, the beautiful Kumba was to be taken to her eagerly waiting husband later in the day.

Jeggan, his companions and immediate neighbours spent the wedding day together in his family home with a splendid meal. His family helped him build a home for his queen. They prepared the bridal quarters well before the afternoon Kumba was expected to arrive.

Kumba Ndaba deserved a home just as comfortable as the one she was about to leave. Jeggan had carefully planned and built the house with help of his family and neighbours.

He had a store twice the size of that of the two families. Their bedroom was very spacious and circular in shape. It was just different from the normal dwelling. He couldn't wait to welcome his bride. Incense was taken from the bark of the Santang tree nearby. It burnt the whole day and night. The room was filled with a pleasant, romantic smell.

Samba's delegation comprising some eminent elders went the next day to bring Kumba Ndaba to her marital home. Jeggan's female cousins went along with drums and musicians in order to accompany the bride to her new home. Nicely made mats were laid under shady trees for the guests.

It was time for Kumba to go to her new home. She got ready to leave. She was led to a small mat placed in the middle of the compound for the farewell advice. It was a hot day. The sun was burning red hot. It was worst than desert temperature of some fifty-five degrees Centigrade. Most of the bees avoided the sunrays whilst the bride was placed under it. She had a thickly knitted honeycomb covering her head. Yet the rays of the sun penetrated through to her scalp. She felt she was being roasted over a fire. She felt uncomfortable. There was no way out for her. She had to bear this first test of resilience.

Kumba Ndaba listening to the farewell advice

The head of the bridegroom's delegation, Saloum
was the first to address the gathering. Standing in the
shade, he said:

"Relatives and friends we are here today on behalf of
the Touray family to congratulate you on the
marriage of your daughter, Kumba Ndaba. The
family has directed us to express our confidence in
the union between Kumba and Jeggan. The couple
has been said to be respectful and helpful to their
parents. We are confident that Kumba will embrace
Samba and Ndeye as her parents and Jeggan would
no doubt do the same. Living together is difficult.
We are confident that we would never hear any
negative comments about the bride from the Touray
family. She would be regarded as a member of that

family. We are ready to take her to her new home. Let us all pray that the Almighty would always guide and protect the couple and their families. Kumba, you are most welcomed to the family and indeed the household."

Baye Ndongo's eldest brother, Jogomae replied thus on behalf of the bride's family:

"Relatives, friends and neighbours I wish to extend greetings to our in-laws who are now an integral part of us. We have maintained very cordial relations with Samba and Ndeye even before Kumba and Jeggan met. It was a long time ago. The marriage between Kumba and Jeggan could only further cement this long-standing and precious relationship. We have no doubts that Kumba would be welcomed in her new home. She would easily become part of the Touray family.

We want to assure Jeggan that he is our son just as Kumba Ndaba is a daughter to Mbissin and Baye Ndongo. Jeggan is well known in this locality as a dutiful and respectable son. We are confident that he would take care of our daughter as he has a good track record of caring for his parents. We pray that this marriage be blessed with many, many children. We know that our daughter is in good hands."

Prayers for a happy matrimonial home were said for the couple. Baye Ndongo's and Samba's sisters, their relatives and friends left their shade. They went to the place where the bride had been seated to lead her to her new home. She had been there under the sun for about two hours. The ladies were curious. They wanted to secretly find out how well the bride had endured the heat of the sun. As she moved away from where she was seated under the sun, they fixed their eyes on the ground.

They were looking for wet spots. Any wetness would indicate that she was not one who would persevere in difficult times. Bees discharged substances under pressure. They were not capable of tolerating high temperatures. Kumba was different. When she stood up, there was not a single trace of wetness on the ground. The female members of her family were elated. They were pleasantly surprised that there was not a single wet spot. They danced with pride. Happy that the ordeal was over, Kumba walked stately as she followed the procession. The group danced and sang:
"Kumba Ndaba,
 Oh, Kumba Ndaba
Oh, Queen of Nayak,
Where can anyone find a more beautiful queen than ours of Nayak?
A bride of real beauty, Ndaba really is
Kumba, oh Kumba
You have shown us, with pride
How resilient you are, Ndaba,
Excessive sunrays left you unscathed, Kumba
The tiniest drop of wet substance didn't ooze out, oh Kumba.

Kumba, Oh Kumba,
You're not afraid of the sun
You will not be afraid of any woman
Oh our dear Kumba, you made us proud and
confident that
You can take the challenge of any woman
You're exemplary, oh Kumba
Take this quality to Tourayen, Kumba."

The drumming and dancing continued until the
procession arrived at Kumba's new home where her
husband and in-laws waited to start a big welcome
party. They were happy that Kumba went through
her first test of time and survived unscathed. She had
been placed under unbearably hot sun to test her
ability to survive under difficult circumstances. She
passed the test.

Chapter Four

Mai's nianyaa get stolen

There was a young, ambitious groundnut trader named Bakary Sanneh. He was a native of the village of Kolong. His dream was to become one of the most successful traders in his area. At the age of twenty-five years, he decided to relocate in search of a big market where he could buy a lot of groundnuts.

One exceptionally beautiful day he bade farewell to his uncle, Lamin who had been his guardian at a very early age when his parents died. He tightly packed all his belongings in a green raffia bag easy to take along with him. He assured his uncle that he would take care of him. He promised him regular sums of money every month. If he were lucky for his business to grow, he would arrange for him to join him in his new home. His uncle feeling deeply satisfied, prayed for him on the day of his departure for Allah's protection, more good luck and the fulfillment of his dreams. The young man then left his small community for a bigger town.

Bakary boarded a donkey cart that was going to the east of the village. The journey was painstakingly slow and uncomfortable as the cart swayed from side to side to avoid the many potholes of the sandy road. The many stops made allowed people to get off at various villages on the way. Thus the journey lasted even longer than usual. Bakary sat patiently day after day. He was grateful for the occasional stops made as rest periods. They were able to stretch their feet.

After travelling for two days the donkey cart reached the populous town of Tubakunda in the late morning of the third day. The soothsayer in Kolong had predicted that Bakary would amass his fortune in a big town east of his home village. Tubakunda turned out to be bigger than he had every imagined. He had never been sure of his destination. When he arrived and saw that Tubakunda was a big settlement to the east, he followed his inner feeling. This town east of his village must be the location that the soothsayer had predicted. This place was going to be his chosen home.

On arrival in the town, which was the seat of the district chief, Bakary asked the first person he met for directions to the chief's compound. A young boy showed him the way. When he arrived at the compound, the chief was engaged in court proceedings. The courtroom was housed in a circular hut furnished with long locally made wooden benches. The hut was in the middle of his compound. People were standing outside by the two front windows. They were looking inside and listening to the proceedings. He too peeped in.

He saw an elderly man dressed in traditional costumes made of cotton damask sitting on a sturdy but opulent chair behind a polished wooden table.

The man was listening carefully to the narrator. I think this must be the chief, Bakary said to himself. It turned out he was right.

Yankuba, as he was called, busy in executing one of his roles as chief of Tubakunda was mediating in a land dispute between two large families in his chieftaincy. Thus he was very attentive. He didn't want to miss anything that was said by the two parties. He fixed his gaze on the speakers.

There was almost no noise apart from the sound of the voice of the person on the stand. Bakary found his way to the door. He hesitated at first. Then he tiptoed to the nearest small space available on a bench and gently sat down. Chief Yankuba's deliberations took long.

Despite the fact that the parties repeated themselves he did not stop them. He was very patient. He allowed them to talk. This helped them to release their bitterness and anger. Bakary was uneasy with the long wait. The wait however, gave him time to evaluate the chief. He did not know what to believe. He wondered whether he would be allowed to settle among the people of Tubakunda.

Thank goodness he had travelled very lightly. If he were to be rejected by the chief, he would try another town in the same direction. He must keep to the direction of the east of Kolong.

Chief Yankuba continued to listen attentively to members of the two feuding families. They eventually stopped talking. The chief wanted an amicable settlement between them as this was about land, which was a sensitive issue. When both parties had fallen silent, everybody looked at the chief. He took the moment to declare his decision. He announced:

"I have listened carefully to what both the Manneh and Njie families had said about the ownership and use of the land that borders their two farmlands. They are both indigenes of this area and have lived together for a very long time. Living together is not easy. It is a known fact that even the teeth and tongue disagree at times. Most of us now know the genesis of the problem. I will not go over it." The chief paused at this juncture and looked around. There was dead silence. He then continued:

"I'm directing four elders of my court to go with members of the Manneh and Njie families tomorrow to the area in question. They would measure the land. It would then be equally divided. The part near the Manneh family farms would go to them whilst the other would go to the Njie family.By the end of this week, a barbed wired fence to be later replaced by a wall would be erected to permanently demarcate the land. It is hoped that would resolve the problem once and for all. None of you should come here again on this land issue. You are allowed to call on me for marriages and naming ceremonies."

There was laughter. The tension had eased. The chief adjourned the court sine die. Everybody stood up and moved towards the chief who was responding to social addresses of other people. Chief Yankuba advised the elders to counsel younger members of their families to accept the decision and exercise restraint. He emphasized the need for peaceful coexistence among people who had lived together for generations. People dispersed. Bakary grew very nervous when he realized he was alone with the chief. It was a scene he would never forget.

Chief Yankuba usually took his break. As he was leaving the hut, he noticed a person walking towards him. He did not recognize the face. Bakary mustered courage, got closer and introduced himself:

"My name is Bakary Sanneh. I was born and bred in Kolong, the little village not far from here. I'm a young groundnut trader. I've been buying the groundnut produce of my people and our neighbours for almost three years. Although I have made many efforts to encourage the farmers of that area to grow more and thus increase their groundnut production, the rise in yields that had been realized was not significant. As a hardworking but ambitious trader, I discussed the issue with my uncle. We examined various possibilities. In the end we decided that the best option was to venture out and try bigger markets. Even though it would mean relocating, it was a risk to be taken. The journey took almost three days but on the approach of the outskirts of this town, I developed hope when I saw hundreds of people working in the fields. On arrival, I noticed the buoyant business atmosphere, an indication of positive economic growth of the town, Tubakunda.

It would be a good place to settle for it is not far from Kolong, my home village where my uncle, Lamin is advancing in age. I must not be too far away from him. He had been very good to me. He took care of me at a tender age when I lost both my parents. It is my personal responsibility to take care of him. I want to make sure that he and his wife would be well provided for. Hearing of my responsibility, which is an obligation, I am hopeful that you would grant me permission as the chief to become your subject. I will do all my best to be a good subject," Bakary appealed.

Chief Yankuba thoughtfully looked at the young man. His explanations showed that he was a considerate and progressive person. He had great respect for old age and sensitive to his duty towards his guardian. It was rare to see the combination of such fine qualities in young men.

When Bakary saw that the chief was silent for some time, he panicked. He thought that the chief did not want a total stranger among his people. Finally Chief Yankuba spoke:

"Bakary, we all know that the people of Kolong belong to this region. We are neighbours and indeed the same people. We have witnessed intermarriage between our two peoples well before you were born and I became chief. Therefore you are our son. You are most welcomed to Tubakunda. This place is also your home. I am confident that if you set up your business here, it will greatly help the people. They will not have to travel to bigger Lumos in order to sell their excess groundnut produce. We will have a big and ready market at our doorstep."

Yankuba's eldest wife entered the room to offer Bakary a cup of cool clean drinking water. The water was freshened by seepah roots. The taste was unmistakable in the water. He quenched his thirst and returned the cup to the woman with nice and well-chosen words of appreciation. When she left, Bakary turned to Chief Yankuba:

"Chief, I cannot express how deeply grateful I am. I must admit my great relief. I was afraid that you would push me away. Your unhesitant acceptance of my request reminded me of my kind uncle. I promise that you will never regret this gesture. I will prove that I am a person worthy of your trust and confidence."

"I'll call my second son Demba. He'll share his room with you. His wife has not yet moved over to live with him. He'll also help you to find your own house and a place to start your business," Chief Yankuba told him.

The chief sent one of the young children playing in the yard to tell Demba that he wanted to see him. Demba immediately came to his father. He was introduced to Bakary. His father narrated what he had promised the new settler. He then tasked him to carry out everything. The chief knew that his son was obedient and would diligently carry out his instructions. Demba left his father and led his guest to his own house.

Bakary explained everything about his life and business to Demba. The latter promised to help him settle down comfortably in Tubakunda. For the time being, they would live together. He took him round the compound to introduce him to all the wives and children of the chief. When they returned to Demba's house, they discussed possible locations for starting the groundnut buying business. Demba proposed that they should inspect all the available places before making a choice. Before that though, they would dispense with an important social norm. Bakary had just come to the town; it was customary that he'd be introduced to the immediate neighbours and the important elders of the town. They decided to do the introductory visits early the next morning. Then they would concentrate on business.

Bakary was amazed by the warmness of the people he visited. He was glad that he had chosen to settle in Tubakunda. The people were friendly. He also realized that they were hard working. Most of them left for their farms after their courtesy visits.

In the early evening, Demba and Bakary went on a stroll purposely to inspect possible places where the business could be set up. There was a big shed in the outskirts of the town. It was not too far from the farms of the people of Tubakunda. Both men agreed to start from the outskirts before inspecting those inside the town. They looked at the shed that was just outside the town. It was big, spacious and accessible to the farms and the main road. But there was a leaking spot on the roof. Both men felt that it was an ideal place. Bakary was willing to mend the roof if the owner was reasonable with the rent.

The shed belonged to Fakebba, a merchant who owned a big well-stocked shop in the middle of the town. They decided to go and see him to find out his plans for the place. It had remained unused for more than a year.

The two young men found Fakebba in the shop. There were other people sitting in a circle with him. In the middle was a wooden stool on which was placed a small canvas laden with cola nuts of different colours. It was apparent that they were partaking of the cola nuts as they chatted. The young men shook hands with each of the elders in the shop. Then Demba spoke:

"Uncle Fakebba, this is my father's guest, Bakary. We've come to see you personally."

"Eh, Demba, I've not seen you for a long time. How's your father? I saw your father-in-law the other day. He told me that they are getting ready for your wife, Teeda to come over very soon. Now what brings you here?" Enquired Fakebba.

"We are looking for a place to start a groundnut buying business and passed by your shed. I have observed that it had been unused for a long time. I thought we should find out whether you'd like to rent it out. Bakary is interested in it," Demba explained.

"I don't have any immediate plans to use it. Since he's your family guest, I'll charge him a token fee as rent. He can pay me two bags of groundnuts every year," Fakebba replied.

The offer was readily accepted. Bakary was set to start work. He planned to recruit some young men who would go to the neighbouring villages to market his groundnut buying business. They would inform people that the business was operating from the shed just outside Tubakunda. Demba would help identify young men who were interested to work with them.

Bakary started work the following day. Demba supported him in every way possible. Five young men from Tubakunda and the neighbouring villages were employed as marketing agents whilst Bakary and Demba bought the produce. The business gradually became known in the neighbourhood. Farmers of Tubakunda and environs no longer took their groundnuts to the Lumos. There was a ready market at their doorsteps.

Bakary moved to a two-bedroom house when Demba's wife moved over. However, the friends continued to work together. Bakary settled down in Tubakunda. He liked the place. The people had accepted him as one of them. He was approachable, businesslike and ready to listen to the views of his workers. Many parents in Tubakunda looked longingly at this clever, mild-mannered and ambitious bachelor for their daughters. He was tall and had a good healthy look. He could be the ideal husband of any lucky and attractive girl. He was respected for his devotion and care to his elderly uncle, Lamin and his wife who had moved over to Tubakunda to live with him. Bakary was never seen in the company of girls. He maintained his distance from them despite his success.

There was a tailor named Sambujang in Tubakunda. He was married to the traditional birth attendant called Lenna. The couple had three children. Their eldest child was a boy named Mafoday. He was eighteen years old. His sister, Mai was two years younger. Their youngest brother, Pa Harley was twelve years. He was fond of following Mai wherever she went. Pa Harley protected his sister just like his favourite toy. It was for a reason. Mai was a beautiful teenager. Men hover around her with longing eyes. She was very desirable.

Mai was aware of her stunning looks. She had a round face, big black eyes and full cheeks. She was of medium built and stood one point fifty-three metres tall. She had a soft expression and when she realized that men were looking at her, she would turn her face to the opposite way to hide a crooked smile. When she chose to meet their looks, those men would wilt under her gaze. She enjoyed being one of the most sought after girls in Tubakunda.

Mai, an only daughter was aware of her responsibilities. She was always by her mother's side helping with the household chores. She took full control of the kitchen and put good food on the table every day. She washed their clothes, cleaned the house and took care of her young brother whom she treated like a baby.

Mai did the family laundry on Thursdays. After completing the laundry, she would take out her nianyaa, wash them clean and hang them to dry. Later she would take her bath, anoint her nianyaa with Shea butter before wearing them again. The removal, bathing and anointing of the nianyaa was a very popular practice among the young girls of those times. They believed that washing and oiling the nianyaa separately from the body made them maintain their firmness and shape. People said that between the first and third days after this gentle care of the nianyaa, they looked different through the girls' short blouses. They were like firm unripe oranges.

The young men especially liked to discuss the way the short blouses sat on the upper part of the girls' bodies. Mai's outfits were eye-catching. She was so beautiful; it was difficult to imagine. Her beauty stunned the senses and annulled reason. No man could resist her. She broke the hearts of many young men of Tubakunda.

The first young man to try to court her was Kebouteh, the second son of Fakebba. Kebouteh helped his father in his shop. He was of medium height and was very good looking. He dressed well and his clothes hung elegantly on him. When he spoke his clear sharp voice resonated some fifty meters away. He was loud. He carried himself with an air of importance and affluence. He narrated the story of his father's success to any willing ear. He was a bluff. He tended to be very choosey and class conscious when it came to women.

Thus when he attempted to woo Mai, he was confident of a warm response. He was hurt by an outright rejection. Mai found him too haughty and full of himself. He decided, though, that he wouldn't give up. He could not see a more eligible bachelor in Tubakunda who should marry Mai.

The eldest son of Chief Yankuba's brother was also interested in Mai. He was an Arabic teacher named Morro. He had the biggest daara in the area with a total of one hundred children. Hence he had to engage two assistant teachers to divide the children into classes. People of Tubakunda and environs sent their children to this school for inculcation of religious education and discipline.

Morro was a disciplined and soft-spoken man. He was very simple in his appearance. He was discreet about his interest in Mai. One day, he paid a visit to the family. Both of Mai's parents, Sambujang and Lenna were at home. He told them that he wished to see their daughter. They suspected his purpose but said nothing. They withdrew from the sitting room so that they could have some privacy.

Mai and Morro were left to themselves. He explained:

"Mai, I know that you'll wonder why I came to see you. I have watched you for some time. I have seen how supportive you are to your mother at home. The whole town applauds you for completely taking over the cooking from your mother. Your brothers adore you because of the love and care you give them. These are rare qualities in young girls of today. I'm satisfied that you'll be a good wife. I came to tell you how I feel about you. Mai, I want you to be my wife. Will you marry me? I don't want to go through a courtship. My desire is to move forward by sending a delegation to discuss marriage with your family."

Mai was not prepared for this. She found it difficult to reject Morro outright. He was too serious and respectable. She paused and then replied:

"I've heard your proposal. It has come unexpectedly and I've got to think about it. Can you give me time to carefully think about it? I'll give you a response in three weeks' time."

Morro did not waste any time. He rose, told her that he would expect an answer and left. His face did not betray any emotions. He went to say goodbye to Sambujang and Lenna and then disappeared. Mai confided in her parents about the purpose of Morro's visit. They listened to her. Her mother was the first to speak:

"So, you told him you wanted to think about it. Hum. I'm sure you already know the type of man you want to marry. Does he fit the description of your dream man?"

Mai was taken aback. She carefully picked her next words:

"I'm…. not sure. He's…too conservative and quiet. I want some one a bit warm and out going. My choice should be good looking also."

"Then he doesn't suit your description. You've made up your mind. Don't keep him in suspense. Let him down gently and quickly too. He would then go and look for a wife. I think that Morro will be a good husband," Sambujang put in.

Mai did not sleep well that night. She kept on thinking about Morro and her parents' words. Although she was not attracted to him, she was yet to meet her Mr. Right. In such a situation, she should be very careful about what to tell him. She'd wait for a week or two before going back to him with a response.

Lamin and his wife watched their nephew Bakary as he worked hard at his shed to expand his business. He left home very early in the morning and returned home late. He was always tired. He would have his dinner and go straight to bed. One night, his uncle, Lamin told him that they must have a man-to-man talk. They went to Bakary's room. The old man was direct.

"Bakary, you can see that with every passing day I'm getting older. My wife and I are very lonely in this compound when you go to work. I'm yearning to see your wife and children. I want to talk to your wife and play with your children before I get too old to handle a child. When is that going happen? You don't seem to have a social life. You spend all your time at work. Please create space for a social life. Identify a nice girl to keep us all company."

Bakary was taken aback. He did not expect this type of conversation from his uncle so soon. When he spoke, he was cautious.

" Uncle, I'll be honest with you. I must admit that I've been engrossed with making a success of the shed. It is true that I've neglected courtship and marriage since I came here. I've not thought seriously about settling down. But I promise you that I'll start looking for a suitable girl as my wife. I have my apprehension about marrying a girl from here. You know I'm not a native of this town. Thus I have to be very careful. Some families might be sensitive about their daughter marrying to a person who they do not know very well. Just pray for me that I'll soon meet the right girl."

Uncle Lamin understood his nephew's concern. He replied:

"Bakary, you're always in my prayers. You'll get one of the best girls in the town.

After this secret conversation, Bakary started to take interest in the social life of Tubakunda. He attended naming and wedding ceremonies. He met girls and watched the way some of them conducted themselves. Mai particularly fascinated him. He had heard people praise her for her devotion to her family. He thought that was a commendable attribute. Furthermore, he found her very attractive. He was not the only man who felt that way. He realized that many young men wanted her. Thus he was in a real fight for her. He was determined to compete with any man for her hand. He knew he had an edge. He was successful and had an impressive appearance. However, there was a down side, which he overlooked.

One evening, he decided to close early from work to visit the chief. It had been a long time since he went to his compound. He was beginning to feel guilty about it. He therefore left with Demba for his home. On the way, they met Mai. They warmly greeted each other. Bakary lingered during their chance meeting. Demba understood that his friend wanted to start a conversation. He addressed her:

"Mai, my wife and I told you about the nicely woven cotton cloths we got from Basse. We're selling them cheaply. I'm yet to see you in our compound. Aren't you interested? I'll tell my wife that I saw you go past our compound."

Mai laughed enjoying the joke. She replied:

"Wrong! Demba, you know I'm interested in seeing the materials. Who will not? Your wife has such a good taste for fashion. I intended to come and see what you have on my way back home. I'm going to buy some salt for my mother from the Moor shop. Don't tell your wife that I'm coming. I want to surprise her. I'll be back soon. Bakary, how's your uncle? I saw him the other day taking a walk with your aunt."

Bakary's spirit lifted. The question surprised but encouraged him to try and know Mai more.

"Uncle Lamin is fine. He's bent on remaining strong. The daily evening walks help him to remain fit. How are your parents?"

"Oh, they're all fine too. If I have to come back quickly, I must go now," replied Mai. She quickened her steps in the direction of the shop.

The chance meeting made an impact. Demba and Bakary walked in a pensive mood towards the chief's compound. Demba felt he had to break the silence. He turned to his friend as he said:

"She's no doubt the beauty of this town. Most of the young men are attracted to her. Perhaps this is confusing her. I don't think that she's made her pick of a man. I noticed you lingered a bit when we met her. Why don't you make a move to attract her? You may be lucky. I can see that you're interested in her. She seems hard to get though."

"Mai is irresistible. I like her, Demba," Bakary replied. His tone softened as he spoke; yet he pretended that he did not want to proceed with the topic. His friend tactfully closed the subject. They arrived at the chief's compound in the quiet mood.

However, the two friends were able to circulate joyfully as they went from one living quarter to another greeting the wives and children of the chief. They lastly went to Demba's house where his wife, Teeda had finished cooking the evening meal. They were comfortably settled to eat a delicious meal accompanied by jolly chat. They had just finished eating when they heard a knock on the door. A soft female voice said:

"Assalamu Alaikum."

"Alaikum Salaam. Come in," replied Teeda.

Mai appeared. Teeda, overcame by surprise, hugged her as she reproached:

"Is it now that you're coming to see my gorgeous and rare lengths of materials? You know, I was angry with you when you didn't come immediately. Now with this surprise I've forgiven you. I'm glad you're here. Better late than never. How are you, Mai?"

"Teeda, I'm really sorry that I didn't come earlier. You have heard that my mother wasn't feeling well. I had too much to do. Can't you see, as soon as she got better, I came? You know I'll come anyway. Eh, Demba! You and Bakary have quickly feasted away the food. Were you afraid that if I arrived too soon I'd eat everything? I take it that my horse couldn't run fast enough for me to miss the delicious food from Teeda who cooks very well," Mai joked.

"Your horse should have galloped faster with a quickened pace. Then you would have been lucky to join us in the meal. We are talking about Teeda's delicious food. Perhaps pretty soon we should confirm another lady's tasty food," Demba teasingly suggested.

"Who are you talking about?' Mai asked curiously.

"No one else but you, Mai," joked Demba.

"You're welcomed. But I'm not competing Teeda. Her food is exceptional. I am but an apprentice to her. I know one thing though. You'll bite your fingers when you taste my cooking." Mai stated with a suppressed smile.

"We'll take you on that. I'll come with Bakary. He's an independent person. He'll be the judge." Demba proposed.

The friends inspected the materials and helped Mai choose a stunning one that had small designs enhanced by golden brown threads running horizontally. Mai left after finding out the cost of the material and payment terms.

Bakary and Demba exchanged glances when Mai invited them to a meal at a later date. Bakary left shortly after Mai. Demba strolled with him until they reached Fakebba's shop and they parted. Two weeks later was the dinner date. Bakary and Demba went to dine at Mai's compound. She had cooked Duurango with chicken and findo. The two men enjoyed it. They were impressed. The conversation was light and hearty. The companionship was warm. Mai's parents were excited. They thought that their daughter had at last made a choice about the man she wanted in her life. They assumed that Bakary was the lucky man. He was eligible and very respectable. He would be a good husband for their daughter. They agreed to wait for Mai to formally introduce him but they knew that there was the other option of Bakary initiating the process by asking for Mai's hand in marriage. He could seek the assistance of his host, the chief to take over arrangements for Mai to be his wife.

Lenna and Sambujang were expectant. They waited for Mai to talk about Bakary. She was not forthcoming. They decided to be patient. Weeks went by. She did not mention anything. Her silence became unsettling. The parents were disturbed. Has she rejected Bakary too? They could no longer hold on to the silence. They summoned their daughter to their bedroom. Lenna spoke first.

"Mai is irresistible. I like her, Demba," Bakary replied. His tone softened as he spoke; yet he pretended that he did not want to proceed with the topic. His friend tactfully closed the subject. They arrived at the chief's compound in the quiet mood.

However, the two friends were able to circulate joyfully as they went from one living quarter to another greeting the wives and children of the chief. They lastly went to Demba's house where his wife, Teeda had finished cooking the evening meal. They were comfortably settled to eat a delicious meal accompanied by jolly chat. They had just finished eating when they heard a knock on the door. A soft female voice said:

"Assalamu Alaikum."

"Alaikum Salaam. Come in," replied Teeda.

Mai appeared. Teeda, overcame by surprise hugged her as she reproached:

"Is it now that you're coming to see my gorgeous and rare lengths of materials? You know, I was angry with you when you didn't come immediately. Now with this surprise I've forgiven you. I'm glad you're here. Better late than never. How are you, Mai?"

"Teeda, I'm really sorry that I didn't come earlier. You have heard that my mother wasn't feeling well. I had too much to do. Can't you see, as soon as she got better, I came? You know I'll come anyway. Eh, Demba! You and Bakary have quickly feasted away the food. Were you afraid that if I arrived too soon I'd eat everything? I take it that my horse couldn't run fast enough for me to miss the delicious food from Teeda who cooks very well," Mai joked.

"Your horse should have galloped faster with a quickened pace. Then you would have been lucky to join us in the meal. We are talking about Teeda's delicious food. Perhaps pretty soon we should confirm another lady's tasty food," Demba teasingly suggested.
"Who are you talking about?' Mai asked curiously.
"No one else but you, Mai," joked Demba.

"You're welcomed. But I'm not competing Teeda. Her food is exceptional. I am but an apprentice to her. I know one thing though. You'll bite your fingers when you taste my cooking." Mai stated with a suppressed smile.

"We'll take you on that. I'll come with Bakary. He's an independent person. He'll be the judge." Demba proposed.

The friends inspected the materials and helped Mai choose a stunning one that had small designs enhanced by golden brown threads running horizontally. Mai left after finding out the cost of the material and payment terms.

Bakary and Demba exchanged glances when Mai invited them to a meal at a later date. Bakary left shortly after Mai. Demba strolled with him until they reached Fakebba's shop and they parted. Two weeks later was the dinner date. Bakary and Demba went to dine at Mai's compound. She had cooked Duurango with chicken and findo. The two men enjoyed it.

They were impressed. The conversation was light and hearty. The companionship was warm. Mai's parents were excited. They thought that their daughter had at last made a choice about the man she wanted in her life.

They assumed that Bakary was the lucky man. He was eligible and very respectable. He would be a good husband for their daughter. They agreed to wait for Mai to formally introduce him but they knew that there was the other option of Bakary initiating the process by asking for Mai's hand in marriage. He could seek the assistance of his host, the chief to take over arrangements for Mai to be his wife.

Lenna and Sambujang were expectant. They waited for Mai to talk about Bakary. She was not forthcoming. They decided to be patient. Weeks went by. She did not mention anything. Her silence became unsettling. The parents were disturbed. Has she rejected Bakary too? They could no longer hold on to the silence. They summoned their daughter to their bedroom. Lenna spoke first.

"Mai, we saw Bakary and Demba some weeks ago join you for lunch. Since then they've not come back. We assumed that you'd made a decision about your future. Most of your friends have got married but you still haven't. Bakary is a fine gentleman and can be a good husband. He's hardworking and very successful. He can easily take good care of you. Any family would be happy to have him as a son-in-law. What happened between the two of you?"

Mai chose her words carefully:

"I agree that Bakary can be a good husband. He has a successful business and can give any young girl all the comfort she desires. He told me that he was interested in me. In fact, he met me again at the chief's compound three days ago when I went to Teeda to give her an advance for that material I took from her on loan. He walked with me all the way to here. He was very clear about his feelings and desire to make me his wife," explained Mai.

"And what was your response?" Enquired Sambujang. He was apprehensive.

"I thanked him for expressing his interest. I promised to get back to him. However, I think he felt rejected. I consciously stared at the deep and ugly scar on his forehead.

That stare left him with no doubt that I didn't like what the scar had done to his face. He stared back at me with horror and bitterness. He turned his back and unceremoniously left," replied Mai with some remorse.

Lenna and Sambujang showed their disappointment by exchanging horrifying looks. They kept quiet. Finally Sambujang found his voice:

"We are really disappointed with you, Mai. What is a scar? Don't you know that even this very moment, you can fall and hurt yourself?That wound could heal and become an ugly scar. Would you be happy if you were shunned by a man because of a scar that is not of your own doing? I thought that you were smarter than what I'm hearing."

Sambujang got up. His wife followed him out of the room. Mai was left alone. She knew that her parents were very hurt. They had dismissed her objection of not accepting Bakary as flimsy. She felt they were unfair to her. Her parents were insensitive to her feelings. They did not even attempt to understand her. She felt let down. She was the one to live with Bakary and she was not sure whether she would get over her misgivings about the scar. The man of her dreams should be handsome, unblemished and of good stature. He should also be successful enough to provide her with all the material comfort she deserved as the beauty of Tubakunda. Mai spent the rest of the day very depressed. She withdrew to her room sulking. Her favourite brother, Pa Harley couldn't cheer her up. When he realized that his sister was not in the mood for his playfulness, he said:

"Mai, I thought I was your best friend in the family but you are not responding to my moves. Am I not your favourite anymore? I am appealing to you to have regard to our relationship and be more considerate with our parents. Remember they also have a right to play with and enjoy their grand children. Please think of that. Right now you don't seem to like the young men in this town. Who do you want then? Are you hiding something from me? Have you someone special you don't want to disclose?"

Mai tried to hide her amusement but could not. She had a soft spot for Pa Harley. Although he was a mere boy, at times he came up with some good ideas. She had been too engrossed with her own feelings and views. She had forgotten that family was very important in society. Traditionally, they played the important role in choosing a life partner in marriage for their offspring. Her parents had allowed her the freedom to choose a husband. They had not showed their preference for any of her suitors. They might show exasperation by her lack of a decision as to who to marry. Perhaps, they were using that to push her to a decision. They should be open to accept her choice.

Bakary on the other hand was mad at Mai. Although she did not reject him outright, he got the dampening message from her eyes. The scar on his face was an issue. He felt hurt and thought very hard on a course of action. He would not accept rejection. He was not a defeatist. Why should a woman reject him because of a scar he had acquired from an accident? He vowed to get her no matter the price.

He would consult his mentor, the elderly wise woman, Nanding who had guided him sincerely since he knew her.

Later that day, Bakary went on a stroll. He took the road to Nanding's home, which was in the inner part of the town. The wise woman was at home. She was sitting under the orange tree. On her lap, she had a small calabash of fresh milk. She was sipping it, enjoying the freshness and taste. She looked occasionally at her four grandchildren who were playing hide and seek. She broke into a broad smile as soon as she saw Bakary. She liked him and found his company delightful.

"Good day Aunty Nanding," Bakary greeted her.

"Hey, Bakary. You know, I miss your company. I was just thinking of you and you walked in. They call it intuition. You think about a person and then he or she appears. Come and sit on this stool near me," Nanding invited him.

The two chatted for the rest of the day. They laughed and gossiped for hours oblivious of time. It was a little after dusk that Bakary rose to go. Nanding walked him to the gate. She turned to go inside and remembered something. She faced him and said:

"Bakary, I almost forgot something I meant to ask you."

"What is it?" Bakary enquired. He was curious.

"Haven't you still seen a good lady for a wife? I've been waiting for you to tell me but I'm tired of waiting. I've decided to ask. Why are you still single?" Nanding asked.

Bakary starred at her. He explained with strong emotions:

"I've tried. I guess you know Mai, the only daughter of Sambujang and Lenna. Everybody agrees that apart from being a beauty, she's a good and considerate girl. She's my choice and I've told her. She hasn't rejected me outright. But when I told her that I wanted her as my wife, I didn't like the way she looked at the scar on my forehead. The look was distasteful. It was as if the scar was nasty. I hated the look and was really angry. But I've challenged myself. She must be my wife no matter the cost. I don't know how I'm going to do that. Can you give me any guidance?"

"Hum. Good old woman's advice. Promise me that you won't tell anybody if I let you into a secret," stated Nanding.
 "I promise," replied Bakary solemnly.

Nanding then confided:
"Mai has her own routine. She goes to the bolong every Thursday to do her family's laundry. She's usually the last person to leave the place. It's

fashionable for girls in this area to remove their nianyaa, clean and then hang them to dry in a secret place. When they are dry, they anoint them with Shea butter before wearing them again. I have had the opportunity to thrice see Mai dry her nianyaa. She hides them between the thick leaves of a daharr tree. She washes them when the sun starts to go down and picks them up just before dusk. You would have to keep a close watch until she is deeply concentrating on packing her clean clothes. You could then take them away. She would go looking for them, as they are the most valuable possessions of girls of this town. We all know how proud they are about their nianyaa. Her search would bring her to your house. That would be the opportune time for you to get her accept your marital proposal."

This was both good advice and invaluable information. He never hoped for anything better. He must carefully plan how to implement Nanding's proposal. He decided that he would start watching the girl on the first Thursday. He could even make a first attempt. Bakary thanked the wise woman profusely and went home. He planned all the way to his house. He was elated by the secret that had been entrusted to him. Nanding was really a true friend, mentor and adopted aunt. He dreamt about getting Mai and tried to figure out how she'd look without her nianyaa. She would have a taste of being in a vulnerable situation.

Two days later, Bakary told Demba he'd like to leave early. He had some important things to do. Demba could continue buying groundnuts during his absence. He was puzzled that his friend had not confided in him. However, he would continue with his work and allow his friend some space. He knew that Bakary would eventually open up to him.

Bakary did not go home. He walked around town and ended at the bolong that was his destination. He noticed that there were only seven women left. He secretly and quietly picked his way to the place that Nanding described to him. He reached it and searched. The nianyaa were nowhere. He had assumed that Mai was among the young ladies that were still at the bolong. He did not check. When he looked at them from his location, she was not there. He had focused on getting the nianyaa. He forgot that the owner should be nearby. Mai must remove, clean and dry her nianyaa. She would then concentrate on finishing her work. Then it would be opportune to take away the treasure. He realized that he had missed in his first attempt. He vowed to be more careful about the small details in his second attempt.

Bakary did not regret the result of his first attempt. It was a learning experience. He had some knowledge of the environment near the laundry and bathing areas. The mistakes would be minimal next Thursday when he would make his second attempt to lay hands on Mai's treasured nianyaa.

Careful planning was Bakary's preoccupation for the next couple of days. He was deep in thought. He decided that for the next attempt, he would go very early and make sure that Mai was at the bolong. He was bent on taking away the nianyaa early in the afternoon. He would not risk implementing his plan in the late evening.

The following Thursday, Bakary excused himself from work leaving the shed to Demba. He lingered a bit near the town market where there were some vendors and customers. The female sellers had their vegetables arranged on pieces of multi-coloured cloth on the floor.

There were half filled bags of rice, groundnuts and coos in front of the corrugated sheds. The men were gathered in twos and threes sharing cola nuts, discussing local politics, as there was only the occasional customer. The sun was moving towards the west. Soon they would keep their commodities in the sheds and go home.

Demba greeted people on his way to the bolong. There were not many people in the streets. People had had their lunch and having their siesta. His timing for the second visit was good. If good luck continued to be with him, he would have positive results. He reached a secluded, green and grassy area, a few metres away from where the women were doing their laundry. In that position, he had a good view of all of the one and a half dozen young girls

They were stooping over big plastic bowls full of dirty clothes. In such positions, their faces were somewhat difficult to recognize. Bakary had a hard time making out the many faces. Who was who?

He moved from one secluded spot to another. He walked, knelt and crawled just to get good views of the faces. He spent his time looking for that particular face, that of Mai. As the young ladies left singly, in twos and threes, he searched and searched. Mai left with the first group of three girls. She had only a few clothes to wash and so finished early.

Bakary did not know that Mai had left. He kept on looking for her. He hoped that Nanding's observation would be true for this day. Mai was habitually the last to leave the bolong. He decided that he would be very patient. He would wait until the last was ready to leave.

Dusk approached. There were three ladies left. They packed their washing bowls and clean clothes. He did not see Mai among them. Bakary was confounded. He could not believe that he had missed her. Possibly, she left early with one of the groups. It might also be that she did not come at all. Exhausted and disappointed Bakary left. Once again he had failed to achieve his goal.

On his way home, Bakary passed by Nanding's house. He needed some consoling words. The wise woman would do that. He was unhappy and wanted some advice. She was surprised to see him. Nanding guessed that Bakary wanted to be alone with her. She led him to her small hut and offered him to sit by her on the bed. He did.

She waited for him to talk. She would take it easy until he was ready to spill out. When he began to explain, beads of sweat covered his forehead. They shone in the light of the glowing candle. He chose his words:

"Nanding, since I left you two weeks ago, I have been on the plan we discussed. I've been to the bolong twice at different times. I've neither seen Mai nor laid hands on her nianyaa. I don't understand how I missed the first two attempts. I know one thing though. I really want her as my wife. I'm afraid that it's divine intervention that prevented me from successfully executing my plan. May be she's not meant for me. I don't want it that way but I fear that's the reason for my failure."

Nanding listened. She knew that deep down in his heart, Bakary did not want to give. That was why he came to her for consolation, support and advice. She spoke:

"Bakary, don't give up so soon. I've seen it in my divinations. She's yours. I presume you've never heard about the saying: 'easy come easy go.' If you want something good, you must struggle to get it. Then when you have it, it would be yours forever.

Just persevere. Make another attempt. You may succeed. This time, you should ensure that Mai is at the bolong. If it means spending the whole day watching out for her, go ahead and do it. You'll get there."

Nanding's words were calming. Bakary's spirits rose. He would try again. He would do as Nanding advised. The whole of the following Thursday would be devoted to executing his plan. He had still not explained the reasons for his absence from work during the past Thursdays to his friend, Demba. He felt that he should wait until Mai accepted his proposal. Meanwhile, it would be a secret between Nanding and himself.

Bakary looked forward for Thursday. The day came. The day before, he informed Demba that he had some matters to take care of. Therefore he would be absent from work. That's the third Thursday, Demba said to himself. I wouldn't ask him until he volunteers the information.

Anxious to finish the business that day, Bakary left around midday. He took the road that led to the bolong. He branched off to a sandy road to avoid being seen by anybody. He came to a small forest area and melted into the natural cover. He was concealed from view but he could see what was happening where the women were chatting and working. His heart raced when he saw Mai walked up to Demba's wife. She gave her one of her washing bowls and returned to where she was drying some of the clothes she had washed.

She turned them over and walked towards the nearby bush. She went to a secluded place where there were no prying eyes. She was there for a long time. She emerged some thirty minutes later. She had changed her clothes. She was wearing a green and white cotton grand boubou. It was difficult to see whether she had her nianyaa on or not.

Bakary suspected that she had taken her bath. He therefore, carefully tiptoed and crawled to the place where Mai had been earlier. He was nervous and afraid of being seen. Yet he was determined to make it. He finally found the nianyaa. They were the only pair hidden among the leaves of her favourite tree. Bakary took them looked at them admiringly and quickly put them in the small bag he had with him. Bakary was partially satisfied. He was also afraid to be seen. He left quickly. He took an unused road back into town.

When Demba's wife, Teeda finished her washing, she told Mai they could go home together. Mai went to retrieve her nianyaa but she couldn't find them.

They had disappeared from where she usually hid them. She called out to Teeda for help. They looked everywhere. They couldn't find them.

It was getting dark and unsafe. After a thorough search they decided to go home. They would alert some of their friends to mount another search the next day.

That night, Mai couldn't sleep. She lay awake wondering how her nianyaa disappeared. It was raining outside. She could hear the wind and the rattling of the rain on the roof. This was one of the longest nights she could remember.

The next day, Mai and her friends went to the bush near the bolong. By then the news of the disappearance of her treasure had spread throughout the town. Most of her friends went with her for the search.They spent the whole morning and the best part of the afternoon looking for Mai's nianyaa. They were nowhere. Exhausted and hungry, they decided that the search was futile. The women were convinced that somebody had stolen them. It was impossible that they would disappear in thin air. Mai cried a lot. She was now unattractive and flat chested. Men of that town admired the size, shape and feel of nianyaa. She had nothing. She felt depressed and hopeless. She withdrew from society and stayed at home. Her family sympathized with her. Even her young brother could not cheer her up.

One night, she stole out of the house. She wanted to find out from the wise woman, Nanding how she could get back her nianyaa. She avoided the main road to Nanding's house. She didn't want anyone to see her. The wise woman was surprised by the late visit from such a young girl. She had heard about the disappearance of Mai's Nianyaa from one of her neighbours. She thought it was the reason for her visit. She would wait though for her to explain.

Mai was a bit confused. She mustered courage and explained:

"Mba Nanding, I've come to see you. By now you must have heard that I lost my nianyaa when I went to the bolong. I have looked everywhere with the help of my friends but in vain. I'm ashamed to go out during the day. My life is in complete shambles. Where can I find them?" Mai wept. Nanding allowed her to cry out her depression.

"Mai, you'll find your nianyaa. I've seen that someone took them away whilst you were busy with your family laundry. I don't know who did it. Do you know anyone who would be interested in your nianyaa? Do you have a fiancé? Have you rejected any men who wanted to marry you? I want you to think carefully." Nanding pronounced. Mai paused. She then revealed:

"There are three men who said they wanted to marry me. One was rejected outright. For the other two, I promised to give them responses later."

"These are men who will be interested in laying hands on your treasure. Go to each of them. Ask them to give you back your nainyaa. Talk nicely to them. I'm sure that the one who stole them would give them back. You have suffered enough." Nanding pronounced.

Mai left hopeful that she would soon find her nianyaa. She was anxious to find her treasure. She decided to start the search immediately. She passed by the compound of her first suitor, Kebouteh on her way home.

May be he would be at home. She would talk to him to let her have her nianyaa back. Thus in reaching his compound, she went to his open window and stood beneath it. She sang:

"Oh, oh, oh, I can't find my nianyaa
 I washed my nianyaa
 I hung my nianyaa
 To dry
Now I can't find my nianyaa.
Where can I find my nianyaa?
Do you have my nianyaa?"

Kebouteh was touched. He felt sorry for the young girl. He had got over the rejection and was about to marry another beauty of the town. He replied:

"Mai, oh Mai
 I've not seen your nianyaa
 I don't have your nianyaa
 I don't know who has your nianyaa

If I had your nianyaa
I'll give them back to you."

From Kebouteh's voice, Mai knew that he was speaking the truth. He didn't have her treasure. Encouraged by his response, she took a chance and went by Morro's house. He was at home. There was light coming from his room. Mai went to the window and sang:

"Oh, oh, oh, I can't find my nianyaa
 I washed my nianyaa
I hung my nianyaa
To dry
Now I can't find my nianyaa.
Where can I find my nianyaa?
Do you have my nianyaa?"

Morro felt sorry for Mai. He had forgotten her after not replying to his proposal to marry her. His reply was:

"Mai, oh Mai
 I've not seen your nianyaa
I don't have your nianyaa
I don't know who has your nianyaa
If I had your nianyaa
I'll give them back to you."

Mai had never felt that Morro would steal her nianyaa. He was too religious and conservative to hurt her. She postponed going to Bakary's compound to the next day. He lived on the other side of the town, which was far away. It was already too late and people had gone to bed.

The next night, Mai sneaked out of their home and went straight to Bakary's home. He had just arrived from work and relaxing in his bedroom. Mai suspected that it was his bedroom window that was open. Bakary's uncle habitually went to bed very early. Mai stood at the window and hummed her song about her nianyaa. Bakary heard and recognized her voice. He ignored her. If she didn't want to talk to him then he won't bother to reply to her question. She hummed her song thrice but there was no reply.

Mai singing to Bakary asking for her Nianyaa

Mai decided to change her approach. She clenched her teeth and sang the song. Bakary still ignored her. She sang thrice but he wasn't moved. He continued to ignore her. Mai was suspicious that Bakary might either be angry with her or had her nianyaa. She entered the compound and stood by his bedroom door. She then sang:
"Oh, oh, oh, I can't find my nianyaa
I washed my nianyaa
I hung my nianyaa
To dry
Now I can't find my nianyaa.
Where can I find my nianyaa?
Do you have my nianyaa?"

This time Bakary replied:
"Oh young lady
I saw your nainyaa
I took your nianyaa
From where you kept them near the bolong
You can only get back your nianyaa
If you would marry me."

Mai repeated her song without answering to Bakary's proposal. He stood his ground that he would not return her treasure until she agreed to marry him. After her third song, she entered his bedroom with this song:
Oh Bakary, Bakary
Give me back my nianyaa
I'll be your wife
If that's your wish

Give me back my nianyaa."

Bakary liked her reply. He swept her into his arms and kissed her. Mai had agreed to marry him. Nanding's prediction about both of them had come true. He gave her back her treasure. She put them on before they went hand in hand to inform their families that they had decided to get married. The most beautiful girl in Tubakunda got married to the most successful bachelor in the town.

Chapter Five

Elephant, Hyena, Snake and Tiger agree to separate

Once upon a time, there were four friends who lived in one compound in the woods of Cassa. Their names were Mr. Elephant, Mr. Hyena, Mr. Snake and Mr. Tiger. They had lived together for a very long time. They hunted and ate together. One night, Mr. Hyena had a strange dream, which troubled him. He woke up and could not go back to sleep. He twisted and turned waiting anxiously for daybreak. When he eventually went to the main room, his friends met him. They noticed his anxious look. They all commented. He told them that he had a nightmare. He expressed the desire for an interpretation of the dream. Therefore, he was going to see the fortuneteller.

Mr. Hyena immediately set out for the home of the soothsayer named Aliwool. When he arrived in his compound, he joined the queue. He waited for over three hours before it was his turn to see the man. Finally he had his opportunity to narrate his scaring dream. The fortuneteller listened to him patiently as he narrated his dream. Then he addressed Mr. Hyena:

The four friends relaxing under a tree

"Your dream is indeed very strange. In fact it is a foreboding dream. It is a revelation of what is going to happen in the near future. The compound you share is going to disintegrate. All of you are not going to live for long, I am sorry to say. You'll all die the same day. This would be as a result of grievous disputes among yourselves."

The interpretation of the dream was very gloomy. It made Mr. Hyena very depressed. He was at a loss as to explain this sad meaning of his dream to his dear friends. He had not narrated the whole dream to his housemates. Yet they supported him in seeking the services of a fortuneteller. He never in his wildest thoughts envisaged that the meaning would be so frightening because of the negative consequences on their relationship. He debated on the merits of

keeping the soothsayer's interpretation secret. He
quickly abandoned that idea. He could not keep such
a threatening interpretation secret from them. He
must be sincere and explain to them what the
soothsayer said about his dream. This would enable
them try to prevent a painful event.

On arrival at their home, he realised that all his
housemates were waiting for him. They were not
only curious but they were also anxious to know the
prediction to the dream. Mr. Hyena was worried.
However, he hid his anxiety and misery by
pretending to be light-hearted about the prediction.
All the four housemates assembled in their main
room to listen to Mr. Hyena's story. He explained
thus:

"My dear brothers,
As you all know, I went to consult the fortuneteller,
Aliwool about my last night's dream. I had to wait
for a long time because there were seven other
clients in a queue waiting for him. You can imagine
my nervousness and discomfort as I waited for my
turn. After waiting for almost three hours, I entered
Aliwool's little room. You wouldn't believe it, I
didn't even have to narrate the dream to him. He
called me by my name with such familiarity as soon
as I entered the room that I was left dumbfounded.
As if this was not enough he went further to tell me
that I had two options. I could tell him about the
nightmare or he could proceed to tell me about it
and its meaning. I was mesmerised.

I half opened my mouth and closed it again. He realized that I wanted to say something. He waited patiently until I found my tongue. This was comforting. With the tension eased, I explained the horrible dream thus:

In the dream, my housemates namely Mr. Tiger, Mr. Snake, Mr. Elephant and I went out on our usual hunt for food. We had roamed very far into unknown territory. There was still no food to be found. Not a single small squirrel crossed our path. We got very hungry.

The normal time for the morning and afternoon meals of the small animals had passed. We never knew that we would ever have to be without food for such a long period. It was much later that our prayer for a prey was answered. A hefty hyena unaware of the presence of ravenous animals nearby tried to run past by leaps and bounds. Mr. Tiger, the swiftest and the fiercest of the group sprang and tore it by the neck.

Let her go! Don't you know that she's my niece? I shouted loudly to my friend. Mr. Tiger paid no heed. He ignored my words. He was deafened by the pangs of hunger.He tore the hyena to pieces. The others, Mr. Snake and Mr. Elephant after sneaking parts of the prey hid behind big trees and grasses to eat their small pieces of the hyena. I was so angry that I stepped on Mr. Snake and crushed his head. Mr. Snake died instantly. Mr. Tiger's eyes turned red with anger. He couldn't bear to see the weakest housemate and friend dead. He eyed me ferociously, a warning that I could be the next on his list for food. I was perturbed yet very resolved to fight back. I had to surprise him. I pretended to walk away. Then I turned and attacked him from the back. Well-meaning Mr. Elephant unsuccessfully tried to separate us. There was a struggle and during it, one of us ripped off the right tusk of Mr. Elephant. Blood oozed out from the wound and this weakened him. Mr. Tiger was enraged. He faced me and sprang. I moved away quickly, he missed me and fell with his full face on a dry tree trunk nearby. His nose bled. I did not escape injury for when I moved away from his attack, I tripped and fell in a deep ditch. I sustained a fractured rib. I moaned with pain and cried for help that never came.

What a dismal sight! All three of us were bleeding profusely whilst one housemate was dead. Fright woke me from my sleep. I sweated profusely. I couldn't go back to sleep."

The other housemates listened attentively to the narration. Mr. Hyena had never given them these scary details. They were getting the real story from him for the first time. They remained quiet when Mr. Hyena finished talking. They exchanged glances before finally turning all eyes on Mr. Hyena. The latter hesitated before proceeding thus:

'Aliwool looked very strange whilst I spoke. His bushy eyebrows appeared crumpled and his eyes squinted. He concentrated on every single word uttered. When I finished, he rose and went to the furthest corner of the room. He came back holding a cow's horn that was adorned with cowries sewn with black thread on a piece of red cotton cloth. The open end of the horn was completely covered with red cloth. There were grey straight strands of hairs glued to the bare parts of the horn. The hairs looked like those of either a lion or a white genii. Aliwool sat down and then placed the horn upright with the sharp edge stuck to the ground. It stood firmly upright. Aliwool spoke to the horn for more than fifteen minutes.

There were responses. They were sharp and detailed. They must be the replies of the horn. The conversation ended. Aliwool kept quiet for more than ten minutes. He fixed his eyes on the horn. Nothing seemed to happen in front of my naked eyes. Slowly he turned and faced me with sadness in his eyes. He cleared his throat. He still kept quiet. Then coming out of the short trance, he very cautiously explained:

'Mr. Hyena!' My heart jumped. With my eyes fixed on him, I listened to him as he continued. I'm afraid I have some sad news for you. I have consulted my genies about your dream. They started their explanation with a description of your home set up. It seems that you amicably live with a snake, an elephant and a tiger. The relationship between the four of you had been cordial for the last five years you have lived together. Although you are different and have your occasional disagreements, there have never been bitter fights amongst yourselves. Sadly, I must say that congenial aspect of the relationship will soon disappear. The four of you will tragically die on the same day. This will happen very soon, sooner than you can imagine. Disturbed by what they said I enquired from the genies for a sacrifice to ward off the tragedy. They came back to me to pronounce there was no sacrifice. They firmly said that they couldn't help. I entreated them to make a concoction that all of you can rub over your entire bodies to stave off any danger. You must have observed that I waited for a long time hoping that the wondrous horn will produce a clay pot full of a protective concoction. Nothing happened. This outcome indicate that what was seen in the dream was predestined. You will all die on the same day. I'm really sorry but I can't save the situation.'

All four friends stood shocked with disbelief. The same thoughts went through their minds. They wondered in confusion how they could all die on the same day. They had lived amicably together for such a long time that they were now family. They could not understand how they could harm each other. That would result in a great tragedy. Mr. Tiger finally broke the silence.

"My dear friends, I'm sure we all have the same burning questions in our minds. First and foremost, it was rather strange that Mr. Hyena didn't narrate the dream to us before consulting the fortuneteller. We do appreciate that he was concerned and confused. However, that did not absolve him from the fact that since we were part of the dream he should have confided in us first. His actions indicate that he had more confidence in a total stranger, a so-called fortuneteller. If he had talked to us, we might have come up with a better solution or even interpretation than what had been offered by the soothsayer. Now that we've heard what Aliwool had said, it would be wise to seek a second opinion. What do you think?"

This was an opportunity to reverse a negative situation into a positive one. All four friends hated knowing that they would die very soon and at the same time. Furthermore, they abhorred going through the agonizing experience of waiting for death. The idea of waking up every morning and wondering whether that was doomsday was too unbearable. They acknowledged the saying that 'in the midst of life we are in death' but they did not want to live with a daily reminder. Mr. Elephant was encouraged by Mr. Tiger's proposal of seeking a second opinion. He endorsed it wholeheartedly.

"You know, I am tempted to forgive Mr. Hyena for concealing the dream. It was a horrible nightmare. It would not have been easy for anyone to narrate it to friends you live with. He chose to tell a fortuneteller whom he anticipated would calm rather than frighten him. We don't know why Aliwool's genies could not come up with a sacrifice to arrest the accident. If they were so powerful, they would have come up with a remedy. I therefore agree that we should consult a more powerful fortuneteller. Perhaps, he would come up with a different interpretation, a positive one."

These words worked a miracle. The despondent mood of the four friends changed. Their spirits were lifted. They finally examined the information they had about all the fortunetellers in the neighbourhood. They agreed to consult a female fortuneteller named Nyahoos. She lived quite close, only five kilometres away. She had a jalang and was known to be very accurate in her predictions. As well as accuracy, many who had bathed at her jalang experienced positive developments later in their lives. They agreed to leave very early the next morning to consult her for an interpretation of Mr. Hyena's dream. They were hopeful that she would be more positive.

The four housemates left early the next morning for the dwelling of Nyahoos. They decided that whilst on their way, they would also look for food for the day. That day the sun was burning hot. Most of the small animals stayed away from the open areas. The hunting idea had a setback. The friends did not mind, as the meaning of the dream was uppermost in their minds. They wanted an interpretation that they could live with. That was urgent. They arrived at the dwelling place of Nyahoos in late afternoon. Her front door was partly closed. They knocked and called out her name but there was no answer.

Mr. Snake crawled in through a narrow gap near the door just to see whether she was sleeping inside. Her bed was empty. They stood at the door. They did not dare to enter the house of a woman with supernatural powers. After some discussions, they decided to wait under a nearby cashew tree. They retreated to it. Soon they fell asleep.

They woke up after the short nap to find Nyahoos sitting under the silk cotton tree opposite her compound. She did not invite them into her house. She just sat on her stool under the tree and looked at them fearlessly. She greeted them and waited for their explanation as to their presence.

Mr. Hyena was leader of the group. He explained to her that they had all come together to seek her wise interpretation of a dream that frightened them. He thought it wise not to mention that they were seeking a second opinion. He truthfully said that he had a dream that troubled all of them. He carefully proceeded to explain the dream. Nyahoos listened attentively. When Mr. Hyena finished his narration, Mr. Tiger informed the soothsayer that he had heard a lot about her supernatural powers. He therefore proposed to his housemates that the best person to consult was she. This was the reason of their journey. Nyahoos remained seated on her stool but was apparently flattered. She then addressed them:

"I feel honoured by Mr. Tiger's words of trust in my powers. My family has always owned a jalang and as I'm the only surviving member of that family, I'm the custodian. I live alone because of my heavy responsibility. That was the reason why when I am out there would be no one in the compound. A few people would dare to enter it whilst I'm away. It was wise of Mr. Snake not to venture beyond the door. If he did he wouldn't come out of the house alive.

Now, with regards to giving you an explanation of your dream, I don't have to go into the house. My genies are always with me. Even under this silk cotton tree they are keeping me company. They are very alert. Thus they have heard all what you have explained. The dream was really terrible. The genies have whispered in my ears that the meaning is more terrible. They have revealed that you will all meet your deaths in one location and more seriously on the same day. The jalang and the genies work hand in hand. They have emphasized in their pronouncements that they won't do anything to change this prediction. I'm sorry that they are unable to help you."

Nyahoos then rose, picked up her stool and entered her house. She did not even look back to see whether the four friends had left. She disappeared and did not return. The housemates were stunned by the similarity of the interpretations of Aliwool and Nyahoos. They were afraid to express their thoughts so near the jalang of the soothsayer. They got up and with heavy hearts quietly left the area.

The tongues of the friends seemed to loosen when they arrived home. They all tried to talk at the same time. They were suspicious that the two soothsayers knew about them and must have consulted each other. The two had hatched a plot against them so that they would separate and stop living together. Mr. Tiger pointed out their weakness. He said that both fortunetellers were loners. Therefore they could be jealous of them. They had lived together amicably for a long time as good companions and had developed a solid bond. Mr. Hyena though was still disturbed by the dream. He courageously proposed that they separate. It was wise for them to take such a step.

Thus they would eliminate the possibility of a bitter quarrel between them, which could culminate in the death of everyone. The lives of each of them were invaluable. Let them all heed the adage: 'prevention is better than cure.' Before they dispersed each of them should announce what he disliked most. This would ensure that they avoided hurting each other. These proposals were accepted by all of them.

Mr. Elephant was the first to start. He disclosed his hatred for any act of disobedience. He especially could not stand anyone who refused to obey his command immediately. When he gave orders the individual must stop whatever he or she was doing. Nobody should ignore his orders.

Mr. Tiger pronounced that he abhorred anyone taking a look at his behind. He could not tolerate that. To him, that act was belittling. Mr. Hyena disliked anyone posing questions to him. Therefore, no one should ask questions to him. Mr. Snake emphasized that he hated anyone stepping on his back. It was dangerous. His reaction to such an act might be fatal to the culprit.

The four housemates separated. They went their different ways. It was a sorrowful parting. They had lived together so long that they had never thought of a separation. They had taken this action so that they would live longer. They agreed to come together from time to time in order to remember old times. It was their destiny to separate.

Indeed the four friends lived separately for some time. They marveled at the fact that they were able to live separately for three years without any mishap. The predictions of the two fortunetellers, Aliwool and Nyahoos did not come to pass. They had registered success in being alive for a long time. They kept to the decision to meet frequently to talk about old times. They did more for they occasionally spent the night together. They had beaten the two soothsayers in their game.

During one of their occasional visits, Mr. Tiger joked that Mr. Hyena had put on a lot of weight. Mr. Hyena ignored the comment. The conversation continued. Mr. Tiger did not take heed of Mr. Hyena's lack of response. He repeated:

"Mr. Hyena, you've put on a lot of weight lately. Look at me I'm starving. I've not got food for the whole of today. Tell me, my friend, how do you manage? Where do you go to search for food? I know that you dislike questions but I don't mean to offend you. I just don't know what to do. Times are really hard for me. Don't you want to share information about food with me? Please give me an idea of where to go to get something to eat."

Mr. Hyena was angry. No matter how the questions were framed, he found them offensive. He had made it categorically clear to his friends that he hated being quizzed. Mr. Tiger had not respected their agreement that they should avoid offending each other.

Mr. Hyena rose from where he sat, went round the other mates and ended at where Mr. Tiger stood. He positioned himself so that he could have a direct view of Mr. Tiger's behind. This was upsetting to Mr. Tiger. He could not understand why Mr. Hyena wanted to offend him instead of sympathising with him in his plight of lack of food.

Hungry as he was, Mr. Tiger turned and ferociously sprang on Mr. Hyena. They fought fiercely. Mr.

Snake and Mr. Elephant exchanged glances. They were shocked by the behavior of their friends. Mr. Elephant who was bigger and stronger than Mr. Snake beckoned to him to stay away from the brawl. He approached his two embattled friends in an attempt to separate them. He shouted at them:

"Mr. Tiger, Mr. Hyena, stop fighting! Have you forgotten the words of the fortunetellers? If you don't stop you will end up killing yourselves. Is that what you want? Do you want the soothsayers to be the ultimate winners? Please stop! Let sanity prevail."

The two combatants were deaf with rage. They attacked each other like bitter enemies. Mr. Elephant went nearer. Mr. Tiger grabbed him by his tusk and gave him a mighty push. Mr. Elephant retreated and mistakenly treaded on the back of Mr. Snake. Mr. Snake bit him before letting out a painful cry. He died instantly. Mr. Elephant was shocked by the death of Mr. Snake. He realised that the predictions of the fortunetellers were becoming true. He had lost his tusk. He was bleeding there as well as where Mr. Snake had bitten him. Yet he was determined to save the lives of Mr. Hyena and Mr. Tiger. He limped towards them and knocked both of them down. Mr. Tiger had weakened from hunger and exhaustion from the long-drawn fight. He was bleeding around his neck. Mr. Hyena also was badly wounded. Both of them lay motionless on the ground for a long time. They bled to death. Mr. Elephant limped out of the area. Mr. Snake's bite was deadly. He was worn-out and feeble. He too fell down and died.

Chapter Six

A Feather for a Goat

Once upon a time there lived an old enterprising woman in the bush of Kassa. She had a small hut whose roof was made of grass. The woman's name was Afaloom. She owned a tribe of good looking fattened goats. Despite her advanced age, she singlehandedly tended her animals. Many who passed by her compound and seen her at work admired her for her strength and impressive animals. One of those fascinated by her apparent wealth was Mr. Hyena.

Mr. Hyena could not contain his admiration of watching Afaloom's animals from a distance. One day he decided to pay a visit to Afaloum. He transformed himself into a charming young man, an appropriate disguise before leaving for her home. As he approached he sighted the elderly but strong looking woman taking care of her goats as usual. She was bent over one of them and did not see the well-dressed stranger. The young man went nearer the compound and stopped at the gate. He greeted her:

"Assalamu Alaikum, Assalamu Alaikum."

" Alaikum Salaam" the old woman replied slowly straightening up to see who was greeting her. She secured her wrapper and looked to her right. She noticed that a young man was standing at her gate. She walked up to him to take a better look at him. Not waiting to be asked in, the stranger entered the compound. He then said to her gently in Jola:

"Kasumai!"

"Kasumai keppe." Afaloum returned his greeting. She closely looked at the visitor as if to assess him. The man went closer to her. He secretly passed his eyes round the compound. He introduced himself.

Mr. Hyena watches Afaloum

"My name is Mr. Hyena." The man adjusted his crispy white starched shirt to seek compliment and endorsement. The woman nodded a sign for him to continue. "I've passed by your compound a number of times and noticed that you're frequently alone. I'm also mostly on my own. But then there's something that is also very important which I think we both miss.

That's friendship. I've always longed for it. It's very important in life. I believe that you and I can do with a solid relationship. Don't you feel lonely at times? It seems that your only friends are your... I mean... your goats. I've come in the name of friendship, which can enrich the lives of both of us. I need a sincere, gentle someone who I can confide in. You are a well-respected elder in the community. I want you to be my adopted mother and mentor. It will be a privilege if you can consider me as your son. I've come with a gourd of palm wine as a token of an anticipated good relationship," the well-dressed stranger explained.

Afaloum fixed her gaze on the man throughout his speech. She thought to herself: he looked impeccable and well mannered. She was impressed by his appearance. His words reminded her of how fortunate she was to have so many goats. So, I'm successful, she thought with great satisfaction. She graciously took the gourd of palm wine from him. She beckoned to him to follow her inside her hut. She invited him to sit on the small stool on the left of her massive bed. She moved to the back of the room and kept the gourd. When she emerged she had a bottle and two cups. She offered him a cup and then poured some of the contents of the bottle in it. Mr. Hyena smelled fresh palm wine and immediately took a sip. Afaloum poured herself a generous cup and sat on her bed to enjoy her drink and the company of her visitor.

Comfortably seated on her bed, Afaloum asked the stranger:
"Now tell me. Where do you come from? Who told you about me? I want to know more about you."

The stranger cleared his throat and began:

"I'm originally from Sumai. My parents had eleven children but they all died before they reached the age of five years. I'm the last surviving child. My father was a palm wine tapper and my mother was a poultry farmer. She had an impressive brood of hens. She reared and sold them to provide food and take care of our small family needs. We were therefore a bit comfortable. I used to help my mother take care of her brood of poultry although I was young.

One fateful day, I decided to accompany my father in the woods. He was well known for tapping wine from the tallest palm trees in the area. He was a good climber. He had on the day before placed his bottles on the tree shafts to get the wine. We therefore went to the bush so that he could remove the bottles. He skillfully climbed the tree to get the bottles that were full to the brim. It was difficult. He had to maneuver carefully so that the contents of the bottles would not spill. He took longer than usual.

The weather unfortunately changed. The sky suddenly went dark. There was a light wind that rapidly grew stronger. Everyone is aware that the weather is very unpredictable during the early days of the month of September. It can rain without any warning. Young as I was, I sensed danger. I called on him to come down quickly. He kept promising me that he would soon descend. He didn't. He was too confident. He was oblivious of the rapidly changing weather. I was really afraid. Suddenly a quick lightning struck. Dazzled with the lightning and fear, I tried to see where it was going to fall. My worse fear happened. I moved away as the lightning struck the tree. A loud thunderous noise followed. I looked to the ground. There was my father's motionless figure, his left hand loosely hold some leaves.

The lightning had broken one of the branches with the bottles. The wine had spilt and wetted his shirt. He had a piece of the bottle in his other hand. He was dead. I stood there stunned. My father was dead. I couldn't believe that the person I was with moments ago was no more. It was the first time that I had seen a dead person. I could not wait for the weather to get calmer before I ran to get my mother. I had to race to her. My mother was home. I didn't explain what had happened.

With great difficulty I asked her to come with me. Fright invaded her eyes when she saw me without my father. She came me with immediately. My aunt and uncle who were spending the day with us followed. I can't express my mother's reaction when she saw my motionless father lying under the tree. The sight was tragic and sorrowful. My mother knelt near his body and with shaky arms lifted the motionless body to her bosom, embraced it and wailed. I cried too. This was the state my aunt and uncle found us under the tree.

With pain but also with strength, they took command of the situation. They got help and took over my father's corpse back to our house. Weeping bitterly, my mother with me by her side went back home where the neighbours had quickly gathered on hearing about what happened. Our lives tremendously changed with the death of my father. The loving, caring husband and father was no more.

My mother mourned him deeply. She gave up living. She neglected the poultry farm, our only source of livelihood. I had to step in to safeguard our livelihood. Six months after my father's death, she too succumbed to death. I was alone in the compound. At the time I was only fifteen years old. I courageously struggled with my late mother's poultry business. My hard work bore fruit. The brood grew bigger.

I employed a young man to help me. Success was beaming on me. I became more comfortable in life. Unfortunately, it didn't last long. Three years after the death of my parents, the poultry farm began to dwindle. The birds were dying in twos and threes. I could not get help. There was a plague that affected all the hens in our village.

Therefore I lost all of mine. Disheartened and rendered poor, I searched for work in the village. I couldn't get any as many families were poultry farmers and so affected by the plague. I had no option but to diversify my choice of looking for a job. I decided to leave the village in search of work.

I moved from village to village in search of one with job potentials. Some two weeks ago, I arrived in this neighbourhood. Siaka, the palm wine tapper was the first person I met. I narrated my story to him. He offered me a small room in his compound. He asked me to stay there until I get a job. I've gone to some poultry farmers but they don't seem to have a vacancy. I'll continue to look for a job."

Afaloum was saddened by the man's misfortunes. She felt sorry for him. She moved nearer to where he was sitting. Holding his right hand, she spoke thus:

"As from today, you can look up to me as your mother. I don't have any children. I have showered all my love to my tribe of goats. I've longed for a son. Now I have one. You're always welcomed to this hut."

The young man was happy. He hugged her to show his gratitude. Deep down, he was satisfied that the old woman was touched. His main interest of getting access to her goats would be achieved with time. He however did not betray such. He pretended that he loved Afaloum as his biological mother. He did his best to nurture and protect their relationship. Every morning, he religiously went to her compound. He helped her take care of the goats. He took care of the sale of the milk to interested customers and brought back all the sale proceeds to her. It was no surprise that she learnt to trust him. The young man went further by treating the goats to fresh luscious leaves of the Kenno tree every week. He would sprinkle these with salt and feed the goats. They got to know him very well. He became a member of the larger family. He was a dutiful son to the old woman.

One day, Mr. Hyena went for a walk. He planned to go and see his adopted mother later. As he proceeded on the walk he came near the bolong where he found a bush fowl whose left wing was broken. It was lying on the beach. It was in acute pain and could not move. Mr. Hyena ran to it. He easily caught it. Happy about his good luck, he decided he would go to see Afaloum.

On arrival at the hut, he held out the bush fowl to her. The old woman's face lit up. She thought that her son had brought it for their dinner. For her, the adopted son could not have been more considerate. He must have been out hunting and felt obliged to bring the bush fowl for them to cook and have a good meal. How mistaken she was in her thoughts. "Keep this for me," Mr. Hyena pushed the bush fowl into her hand.

"Hey, no. Isn't here your home? You know the place very well. You can therefore go and keep it for yourself. No one will touch it once I'm here," replied the shocked and disappointed old woman. She refused to hold the fowl.

The young man went out with bird in hand. He hid the bush fowl in a covered spot with a post in the vegetable garden. He then returned to the hut to chat with Afaloum. After some time, he started complaining of hunger. The old woman ignored him. Hurt by Afaloum's attitude, he left the room without telling her where he was going. He went to the vegetable garden where he had secured the bush fowl to the post. He grabbed and killed it. He ate some of it. He carefully cleaned his mouth and returned to Afaloum's hut. They continued chatting. None of them mentioned the bush fowl. Just before dusk, the man took leave of the old woman. He explained that he had an appointment with Siaka and must leave in order not to be late. He went away.

Mr. Hyena did not stay away for long. He did not trust Afaloum with the remainder of the bush fowl. He believed that she would look for it and cook what remained of it. He therefore hurried back to Afaloum's hut. He asked her for his bush fowl. She replied indifferently:
"Go over there. It should be where you kept it." She pointed to the direction he took earlier when he wanted to keep the bird. He went to the garden and found the half eaten bird as he left it. He ate every

bit of what was left. He then departed without the courtesy of saying goodbye to the old woman, his adopted mother. Afaloum was startled by his sudden change of attitude. The young man was behaving strangely. Just after darkness fell, Mr. Hyena rushed to the old woman's house panting, as he called out to his adopted mother.

"Afaloum, Afaloum, where's my fowl?"

"It should be where you kept it. As it is rather dark it might be difficult to see. But it should be there. No one entered this compound since you left," replied the old woman perplexed.

"I can't find it. It's not here. Did you take it?" Mr. Hyena said in an agitated and irritated voice. With this mood, he ransacked the whole compound thus waking up the goats. He kept on shouting out wickedly:

"Somebody has taken my fowl. I kept it in your compound and it's disappeared. Afaloum, kalim dou Johla. You must pay for my bush fowl. And let me tell you, you'll have to pay me a goat for every feather."

Afaloum was dismayed by the aggressiveness of the young man. Her adopted son had become an unknown stranger. She could not believe that this was the very nice young man she had adopted as her son. He had always been so courteous to her and helpful with the goats. She could not believe that the same person was making such a demand on her in this rude way. She thought about his words and tone. She was frightened. It was late and the place was really dark. She was old and helpless. If she did not concede to his wishes she could see worse. She did not have an option except to satisfy his demand. Gripped with fear, she said to him:

"I know that you kept your bush fowl in my compound. Although I did not see where you left it, this is my home. I would take responsibility for your loss. Let's go to the shed. Your demand is for a goat, I'll give you one."

Mr. Hyena and Afaloum went to the sleeping animals. She untied a big goat from where it was bound and handed it over to him. She felt that would nip the problem with him from the bud. Happy, Mr. Hyena removed the rope. The goat followed him meekly. He had a good meal from it. He left some of the goat's meat for the next day.

The following night, Mr. Hyena sneaked into Afaloum compound. She was not expecting him for she'd not seen him that whole day. When the old woman saw him enter the hut, she was terrified. His attitude was hostile. He addressed her again on the disappearance of his bush fowl:

"Ah, ha! Afaloum, Afaloum, I've come. Ha, ha, ha! Kalim dou Johla! You still owe me. It's a goat for each feather. Remember? I've come for debt collection. Where's the goat? I'm in a hurry. Let me have it quickly."

"Is this the way you behave towards your adopted mother? Have you come to deprive me of my tribe of goats? Okay, I'm old and weak. I can't resist if you decide to be forceful. You know full well that the goat I gave you last night is a handsome payment for your wounded bush fowl. Since you are insisting, I'll give you another goat. Follow me to the shed," replied intimidated Akaloum. She had become afraid of the young man. He had become a real fearful stranger. This time, she did not choose the best. She took the goat that was nearest to where she stood and handed it over to Mr. Hyena. He did not care. He had made up his mind to demand for one every day and so finish all her goats. He would get the goats in whatever order she delivered.

Mr. Hyena wickedly carried out his nightly visits and demanded for a goat on each. The old woman's situation became pitiful. She had lost all her goats except for one. She no longer had a source of income. She became worried, nervous and very depressed. She was afraid of her adopted son who had become a changed man and had taken away her goats. She had nowhere to go. She had no one to confide in. She was no longer busy. She spent the day sitting on a small bench in her verandah gazing in space as time passed by.

One day Mr. Hare passed by. He was going to pay a visit to his mother. He was surprised to see the once busy old woman looking sad and idle. He noticed that there was only one goat in the compound. He could not resist finding out from her what had happened to the others.

"Assalamu Alaikum, Afaloum. How are you today? You look very miserable. Is anything wrong with you?"

"Alaikum salaam, Mr. Hare. I'm not fine at all. Can't you see? I've aged a lot lately," Afaloum replied pitifully.

"I can see that. But where is your tribe of goats? You have only one in the shed today," Mr. Hare observed.

The old woman explained how a stranger had come to her with a very pathetic story. She was touched by it. She felt sorry for the young man, the stranger who revealed that he was orphaned when he was a teenager. Her pity made her to adopt him as her son. A good relationship was built. In the beginning, the young man was very helpful and dutiful to her. He was by her side daily tending the goats.

One evening he came to see her holding a wounded bush fowl in one hand. He asked her to keep the fowl for him. She told him that as he was familiar with the compound he could take it for safekeeping anywhere. He did. He hid it in a place that he alone knew.

During one of his visits, he claimed that the fowl had disappeared. He confronted her, his adopted mother with a strange demand. He said that she had to pay for his loss because the fowl was kept in her compound. He demanded a goat for every feather of the disappeared bush fowl. It was in this way that her cunning adopted son tricked her into giving him all her goats. Now she had only one goat left. She was afraid that he would very soon come and claim the last goat.

Mr. Hare was sympathetic. He was however angry that this young man would take advantage over a productive but naïve and harmless old woman. Mr. Hare then proposed to Afaloum:

"Let's go to Mr. Lion who's the king of the jungle. I suspect that you've been tricked by Mr. Hyena whom we all know very well. If you explain exactly what you've told me, Mr. Lion would want to help you. He could even take on Mr. Hyena singly handedly. He'll easily stop him from taking your last goat. If Mr. Hyena isn't taught a lesson, he'll turn you into a pauper."

The two went together in the forest in search of Mr. Lion. They found him resting under a big mango tree. Mr. Hare narrated the story of the old woman and how an adopted son who turned out to be Mr.

Hyena had tricked her. Mr. Hyena had eaten all her goats and she was afraid that he would soon ask for the last one.

Mr. Lion listened attentively. They then discussed how to stop Mr. Hyena from taking away the last goat. They agreed to Mr. Lion's prudent proposal. Mr. Lion would go to Afaloum's compound at dusk. He would hide in the garden until nightfall. Then Afaloum would tie him to the post where she usually secured her only goat. They would patiently wait for Mr. Hyena's visit. If he didn't visit that night, they would repeat their plan until he came. With such a plan, they were bound to catch the rascal.

When the sun went down, Mr. Lion went to Afaloum's compound. He waited at the back of the hut until it was pit dark. Then Afaloum took him to the shed. She bound him to the post in the shed. She then took the sleeping goat into her hut. Mr. Hyena visited that night. He arrived a few minutes after Mr. Lion was taken to the shed. He called out: "Ha, ha, ha! Afaloum Afaloum! Kalim dou Johla! Where's my payment? Remember? It's a goat for each feather. I've come for the goat."

He entered the compound in an aggressive manner. He wickedly demanded for the last goat from her. Afaloum pretended to reject the demand. He became nasty. The old woman pretended as if she had given in. She invited him to go with her to the shed where she kept her only goat. She untied the rope and as she handed it over to him, said tearfully:

"My son, this is the last goat in my possession. You've taken away everything that I've worked so hard to own. You came to me as a well-behaved young man looking for a mother. You are leaving me tonight as a complete and hostile stranger. You've thoroughly wrecked me. I hope that you're now happy that I'm a pauper."

She turned her back and headed for her hut. Mr. Hyena laughed wickedly. He led the goat away. They had gone half way. He listened to the noise of the walking goat. That's strange, he thought. It's different from the noise of the other goats that were led away from the old woman. The noise he heard sounded as if coming from paws. He wondered whether the old woman had played a trick on him. He stopped to look more closely what was behind him. He stepped on paws.

"Ha, ha, ha, you wicked trickster! You thought that everything would go the way you planned it. Well this time you've got me. Go ahead and slaughter me for your dinner," jeered Mr. Lion.

As Mr. Lion spoke, Mr. Hyena dropped the rope and turned to escape. Alas, he was not fast enough. Mr. Lion sprang on him and tore him to pieces. Mr. Hyena was the dinner of Mr. Lion that night. A well deserved end.

Chapter Seven

Mr. Hyena and Mr. Hare live together in one home

Once upon time, animals living in the thick forest of Foni developed very close relationships. The harmony that existed was so good that they peacefully lived in the same dwelling place. It was rare to hear of big ferocious animals eating the small ones out of need.

In such an environment lived two friends named Mr. Hyena and Mr. Hare. They were known to be very intimate. They set up their home in an area of the forest that was covered with lots of palm and cashew trees. They hunted and ate together. In most cases when they went out, Mr. Hyena took up the responsibility of securing food. He would make all the effort to get the food they needed. He dutifully fed their two families. Mr. Hare took it easy. Since he was assured that he wouldn't go hungry, he had no cares. This wasn't to last. Mr. Hyena noticed the carefree attitude of Mr. Hare and felt it should cease. One morning Mr. Hyena made a proposal:

"My friend, I've been thinking lately about the ways we get food. Have you noticed that when some of the very small animals see us together during our food finding missions, they hide or run away? This is why it has been difficult for both of us to get food when we are together. I think it would be wiser if we separate. On such days, you can go one way and I will take another route. Then we can meet here in the evening and share our dinner."

Mr. Hare was taken aback. Yet he cleverly masked his surprise with these words:

"I agree with you Mr. Hyena. I'm ashamed of myself. I have not done well at all. During the last month, I didn't even catch the smallest rat to offer for food. It is a shame that I've failed to put food on the table. It's not a nice feeling to be over dependent. Let's try what you have proposed. Perhaps, I'll be lucky to have some catches for dinner."

The next day they went their separate ways. Mr. Hyena as usual went out hunting. Mr. Hare decided differently. He would establish a farm. He was sure that if he planted corn and coos, he would have food for a whole year. He was more concerned with what he would need to eat. He did not think of the common interest.

There was a big and shady cashew tree near the area that Mr. Hare wanted to set up his farm. He took this tree as the demarcation between his farm and that of Mr. Fowl, a fellow inhabitant. He decided that when he felt exhausted he would go under the tree to rest and even take a nap.

As soon as he arrived in the area, Mr. Hare started to clear the plot of land. It was very tasking. He took a break when the sun was directly overhead. He was thirsty and feeling the hunger pangs but he managed to ignore them. He willed himself to wait until the evening before searching for food. As he approached the cashew tree, he saw something. It was reddish brown in colour. It was not moving. He hesitated. Then his curiosity forced him to move nearer. He felt foolish. How could I feel intimidated by a cooking pot? He said to himself. Probably one of those female farmers had abandoned the pot because it had a small hole. Those women were fond of bringing their cooking pots at their farms to cook their midday meals in turns. He got brave enough to look at the pot pitifully and said aloud:

" Oh, Pot, I'm really sorry. These women used you until they were tired and then abandoned you. You must be very lonely here. Did one of those women make this hole in you? You still look beautiful to me though."

The pot replied feeling flattered: "Do you really mean what you said? Do I look beautiful? I'm happy that those women have gone. I've yearned for moments when I wouldn't be troubled. No one would misuse me by cooking and cooking non-stop. You know, these women overused me. As a result I hatched a plot. A little hole developed at the lower side. I kept on leaking water into the fire and this put it off during cooking. It therefore left the women without lunch. They thought I was damaged and disposed of me, as I was no longer useful to them. I was happy to get my freedom. You see, now I can take good care of myself. I've nothing to do. But coming back to you, you said I looked pretty. Did you really mean it?"

"Yes, I mean it. You look so different from the other pots I've seen in many homes of people. Since you are so pretty, may be you can tell me how useful you can be to me. Here I am tired, thirsty and hungry. Tell me, where can I get something to eat and drink?" Mr. Hare asked.
The cooking pot laughed.

"Well, well. Is that all you are asking? That's easy to respond. I can cook you a delicious dish. You'll always come for more when you taste my food. By the way, my name is Mrs. Pot. " The pot added.

"Oh, I must not forget to introduce myself too. I'm Mr. Hare. Now, let us not spend too much time on greetings. Can you please help me with some food? I'm famished. Quickly do any dish," stated Mr. Hare as he lay under the tree. He was not convinced by Mrs. Pot's claims. He eventually fell asleep. He must have been in the middle of his nap when Mrs. Pot called out to him:

"Mr. Hare, Mr. Hare. Your lunch is ready. Please come and eat."

Mr. Hare heard this sweet melodious voice like that of a young woman. Quite dazed, he opened his eyes a little. He must be dreaming. He turned over his position and lay on his left side. Something touched him on the tail. It was a gentle pull. He forced open his eyelids and peered at Mrs. Pot. She was full to the brim with a steaming thick vegetable soup. Mr. Hare sat up. He could not believe his eyes. He licked his tongue as saliva dripped to the ground. He approached the steaming pot to take a better look at what was in it. He took the big spoon that was hanging from the pot and tasted the food. It was delicious. He sat down to drink more of the soup. He had to satisfy both his hunger and thirst.

When Mr. Hare had had enough, he thanked Mrs. Pot and returned to his work. He bent over to start his work but his stomach did not allow him. It was too full. No matter which position he took, he could not reach the ground.

"Ah, well, I've done a lot of work during the first part of the day. I can stroll to our home so that this food would digest. I'll then come back and work until the sun is down. Mr. Hyena would be on his way home by then," he said to himself.

Mr. Hare went home. He had over eaten and felt drowsy. He went to his room for another nap. He woke up feeling guilty that he had not completed what he was supposed to do at the farm. He ran to the place and resumed his work. He successfully finished clearing the farm before the sun went down. As he was leaving the farm, Mrs. Pot arrived. Mr. Hare was pleasantly surprised and declared:

"You almost scared me to death. I thought you had gone home. What are you doing here? You've fed me so well for which, I'm really grateful. Do you need a favour from me?" Mrs. Pot amazed, said sweetly:

"Oh! I am honoured by your kind words. But I've come to invite you to dinner. See, I've cooked a wholesome chicken soup for you. Would you like to have some?"

"You're tempting me. Of course I would. Who wouldn't want an enjoyable and delicious dinner?" Mr. Hare replied pleasantly with a laugh.

He did have his fill from the soup and left for home empty handed. He did not even think of taking some for Mr. Hyena. He didn't consider it was his business to care whether he ate or not. He was not worried for he knew that he could always provide answers to his friend's questions.

Mr. Hyena was at home when Mr. Hare walked in. Mr. Hyena looked at his friend. He saw that his friend had again returned without bringing dinner. He never makes an effort. Mr. Hare likes to depend on me. What should I do? Mr. Hyena debated within himself. His eyes betrayed his disappointment. His friend had let him down. He had to scavenge in dustbins for bits and pieces of well-chewed chicken bones. They were hardly enough for him much more sharing with his friend. They ate what they had and went to bed. Mr. Hyena was still hungry when he retired for the night. Not so for Mr. Hare.

The next day, Mr. Hyena went hunting whilst Mr. Hare set out for his farm. Mr. Hare met Mrs. Pot near the cashew tree.

"Good morning Mrs. Pot. How are you? Thank you for that nice dinner yesterday. It helped me to easily go to sleep. You know it is difficult to sleep on an empty stomach."

"Oh, Mr. Hare! It's a pleasure to feed you. I don't have much to do any way. If you need me, just sing this song and I'll bring you some food," Mrs. Pot stated.

"What's the song? Sing it for me. You know, I'm very good at memorizing." Mr. Hare said excitedly:

"Mrs. Pot, Mrs. Pot
 My beautiful lady
 I've never seen such a Pot
 That feeds
 The hungry on any day
Fill their stomachs with delicious food
 Delicious is her second name."

Mr. Hare was thrilled. The words sounded like music. He pleaded with Mrs. Pot to teach him the song. He quickly mastered the words after five repeats. On that Mrs. Pot left. Around midday, Mr. Hare decided to take his usual break. He had by now been used to midday meals. As agreed, he went near the spot he met Mrs. Pot and sang:

"Mrs. Pot, Mrs. Pot
 My beautiful lady
 I've never seen such a Pot
 That feeds
The hungry on any day
Fill their stomachs with delicious food
 Delicious is her second name."

Mrs. Pot appeared full of appetising rice and chicken stew. Mr. Hare started to lick around, the mouth dripping with saliva. He appealingly invited Mrs. Pot under the tree where he felt was right to eat. He slowly ate savouring the delicious meal. As he ate Mrs. Pot chatted with him on the admirable progress he had made on his farm. He had planted good seeds that were gradually growing into healthy plants. He lapped up the admiration as he ate. He waited until finished eating the food before addressing Mrs. Pot thus:

"You know I'm beginning to feel guilty. I have not been useful as a sign of appreciation. Whenever I finish eating I don't even help to wash you. I want you to allow me to do that at least as a thank you."

"Ha, ha, ha!" Laughed Mrs. Pot. "You must be joking. Have you ever heard of an animal washing a pot? No, Mr. Hare! I won't be the guinea pig. I'm comfortable doing it. I enjoy taking care of you. If you need me, you know how to reach me. Good bye." With these words Mrs. Pot disappeared.

After his short siesta, Mr. Hare resumed his farm work. By late evening he decided to close for the day. However, after the hard work of the afternoon he must have his dinner first before going home. He reverted to the song:

"Mrs. Pot, Mrs. Pot
My beautiful lady
I've never seen such a Pot
That feeds
The hungry on any day
Fill their stomachs with delicious food Delicious is her second name."

Mr. Hare was patiently expectant. Mrs. Pot promptly appeared with his favourite okra soup. The okra soup was tasteful and he ate everything very quickly. Mrs. Pot admired Mr. Hare's huge appetite. She had never come across an animal or human who could finish a pot full of food within so short intervals. She attributed this to her appetising food. It also confirmed her as a good cook. She could challenge any female human or animal in the art of cooking. She marveled giving food to Mr. Hare.

Belching loudly, Mr. Hare struggled to stand.
Gradually he steadied and then sluggishly headed for
home early that day. He had enjoyed his favourite
okra dish. He had eaten greedily. He felt very heavy,
lazy and sleepy. Yet he was able to enter their abode.
He had enough strength to bellow, 'Mr. Hyena! Mr.
Hyena!' There was silence. He proceeded to his
housemate's part of the dwelling but he was not
there. He assumed that his friend was still in the
bush looking for food. He retired to his own
quarters and immediately fell asleep.

Mr. Hare snored so loudly that the neighbours
thought that the noise was coming out of the house
as a result of a fight between the two friends. They
rushed to the house to save the weaker one. They
felt they should when they saw Mr. Hyena enter their
dwelling. The sight of all the neighbours hanging
around took Mr. Hare aback. He enquired whether
something terrible had happened to friend. Not
waiting for an answer, Mr. Hyena rushed directly to
Mr. Hare's quarters. The neighbours waited outside.
Mr. Hyena to his dismay, found his friend in a deep
sleep. Very relieved he muttered the prayer "Thank
God, he's safe".

Mr. Hyena gently nudged his friend on the stomach
in an attempt to wake him up. When he touched his
friend's stomach he realized that it was full and tight.
He said to himself: my friend must have come across
a lot of food. He generously helped himself. I can
feel the fullness of his stomach.

As if he sensed the presence of someone, Mr. Hare drowsily opened his eyes. He realised that Mr. Hyena had returned home after a long day. He could not understand why his friend should disturb him after a tedious day. He had come home early and was already retired in bed. Why didn't Mr. Hyena respect his need to be left alone peacefully? Irritated by his friend's lack of consideration, Mr. Hare angrily said:

"Why are you waking me up? Don't you see that I'm already in bed? I've had a long and tiresome day and need some rest. You had an easy time just hunting. I do a difficult job. Weeding a farm is no mean job. Now, leave me alone."

"I won't leave you alone. The whole neighbourhood is outside. They hailed to our dwelling for they thought that something had gone terribly wrong between the two of us. They mistook your loud snores for cries arising from a fight between us. Now that you know why I woke you up, you must tell me why you made such loud noises during your sleep. I have noticed that you've been putting on weight lately. On the other hand I've got thinner and thinner. More importantly you've never been concerned about dinner when we are together in the evenings. I've always struggled for food. It seems you don't. Where do you get it? Come on spill the beans out. I'm now going out to tell the neighbours that nothing is wrong and you're fine. On my return you'll have to tell me everything."

Mr. Hyena went out. He informed the crowd that the noise they heard was Mr. Hare's snores. The neighbours all heaved sighs of relief and left satisfied that there was peace. Mr. Hyena then went back to his friend's room. He stood directly in front of him and looked into his eyes. Mr. Hare cowed from the spell of the piercing looks of Mr. Hyena explained in a tight voice:

"Okay, okay. If you want to know where I get food everyday come with me to my farm in the morning. You'll have to help me with the work. Remove the weeds and drive away the birds. " The invitation was accepted.

The next day, the two friends set off early for the farm. Mr. Hare made Mr. Hyena work really hard. He cunningly divided the farm between them with the larger part for weeding going to Mr. Hyena. Weak and hungry, Mr. Hyena persevered and worked with determination. He didn't want his small friend to think little of him. At noon when the sun was directly overhead, Mr. Hyena observed that his friend Mr. Hare was pretending to be doing some work behind the cashew tree. He heard his voice loud and clear. He looked for but was unable to see with whom his friend was talking. He decided to find out. He, Hyena did not trust him. To his surprise, he found a pot full of soup and meat in front of Mr. Hare. The latter, somewhat embarrassed had to say:

"Come, Mr. Hyena. It's time for lunch."

Hyena accepted the invitation. He went beside Mr. Hare. They ate in silence. Mrs. Pot was quiet. They finished the delicious food and lay down to rest. The fullness soon sent Mr. Hyena to sleep and he snored loudly. Sure that he was in a deep sleep, Mrs. Pot prudently sneaked away. She did not want Mr. Hyena to know her identity.

Mr. Hyena woke up and unaware of the disappearance of Mrs. Pot went back to his work. He did not disturb his friend Mr. Hare who continued to sleep. A little later, Mr. Hare woke up to see his friend hard at work. Both of them were well fed and energised. They could finish the work they had earmarked for the day. Some five hours later, Mr. Hare retreated behind the cashew tree. He did not know that Mr. Hyena was listening carefully. Mr. Hare sang the magic song that summoned Mrs. Pot. As the song tailed off, Mrs. Pot emerged oozing out a nice steamy smell from the top opening. Mr Hyena could sense the presence of food. He remembered their lunch. He suspected that his friend was about to have dinner. He did not wait to be called. He hurried to the spot where his friend was busy talking to Mrs. Pot and said:

"So, Mr. Hare, this is the secret you've been hiding from me all this while. I've heard the magic song, which empowers this pot cook the wonderful food you've been enjoying. I thought that as friends we should extend goodwill to each other. But I've seen that you don't place value on our relationship. If you did, you wouldn't have allowed me to starve when you were having plenty to eat. But let's not allow the food to get cold. Let's eat. You would never be able to give me a good reason why you shut me out of your life for food."

Mr. Hare was indeed embarrassed. He would never be able to give a convincing explanation. He opted to sidestep his friend's accusations. They ate in uneasy silence. When they finished, they started their homeward journey. Still, they did not speak to each other. All the way, Mr. Hyena secretly planned how to get the correct words of the song from his friend. He had a bargaining chip. His friend had not been true to him and there was sufficient proof. He could use that as blackmail against him. Mr. Hare would be forced to teach him the words. It was obvious that Mr. Hare was very uncomfortable as they walked side by side silently to their home. He wondered what his friend was plotting. He guessed that Mr. Hyena would want to know the secret behind the relationship between him and Mrs. Pot. How soon this would be disclosed through a demand was anyone's guess.

The request came sooner than Mr. Hare expected. Next morning on their way to the farm, Mr. Hyena boldly broached the subject.

"My dear friend, forgive me for the harsh words I used yesterday. I felt betrayed. I couldn't imagine that you would leave me to starve whilst you feasted.

It was unbelievable. I was very hurt but after a good sleep I've got over it and now that I know the secret, you will feel obliged to teach me the song. I promise I would only use this means of getting food when I'm really in a desperate hungry condition. Otherwise, I'll leave all food matters in your capable hands. After all you discovered Mrs. Pot."

Mr. Hyena sounded very forgiving and convincing. Mr. Hare, though knew that his friend would not keep his word. He was, however, in a weak position. He had no option but to yield to the request to teach him the words and pray that it would not be misused. The singing lesson started immediately and by the time they arrived at the farm, Mr. Hyena had mastered the words. He was happy that he could at last sing the song. He was determined not to use it in Mr. Hare's presence. That whole day, Mr. Hyena in his effort to assure his friend of his reliability kept his distance and allowed his friend to take care of the meals. This was not to last.

Late that very night, Mr. Hyena sneaked out from their dwelling and returned to the cashew tree. He was desirous to test whether Mrs. Pot would respond to his call. He sang the song. To his utter surprise, Mrs. Pot came full of thick steaming meat soup. He ravenously drank the soup. Mrs. Pot was not surprised that Mr. Hare's friend had come. She had been suspicious of him from the start. Nevertheless she vowed not to tell Mr. Hare anything since Mr. Hyena was his close friend.

With a full stomach and satisfied that he succeeded in carrying out his secret mission, Mr. Hyena returned to his living quarters. He sat next to his wife and wasted no time to confide in her on his good fortune.

"My dear, when we wake up tomorrow, break all your cooking pots. You don't have to cook any more. There would be no need."

Mrs. Hyena sat up. She couldn't believe her ears.

"What do you mean? Why should I break all my cooking pots? Are you out of your mind? You've come up again with your dream ideas. If I break them and your plan doesn't go through, what would happen to us?"

"Why do you always have doubts? This one is different. We will try my plan at dawn. We'll go for breakfast. Seeing is believing." Mr. Hyena proposed and Mrs. Hyena agreed.

Mr. and Mrs. Hyena sneaked out very early the next morning. Mr. Hyena led his wife to the spot under the cashew tree and sang the song. The wife stood dumbfounded when Mrs. Pot came full with some nicely cooked mixed meat grill. It looked appetising. Mr. and Mrs. Hyena wasted no time and had their fill. They finished the food and left quickly before Mr. Hare set out for the farm.They returned home unseen.

From that day onwards, Mr. Hyena stopped going to the farm. He always had an excuse. Whenever his friend returned home from the farm and retired to his quarters, Mr. Hyena and his wife would go to the area and sang the song. Mrs. Pot would appear with the food. Thus Mr. and Mrs. Hyena had meals free and with ease.

With time, Mr. Hyena got fed up with playing 'hide and seek'. He had been avoiding an accidental meeting with Mr. Hare and Mrs. Pot. He decided that at their next trip, he would take the pot to his dwelling. This would put an end to his secret trips. He would hide the pot and sing the song in a low voice. Thus he would monopolise securing the good food that they had all been enjoying.

Mrs. Hyena places pot on Mr. Hyena's head

At the next dinner with Mrs. Pot, Mr. and Mrs. Hyena ate all the food. Then Mr. Hyena asked his wife to help him put the pot on his head. They struggled for over an hour. The pot kept moving from one side of his head to the other. It refused to rest in one spot on the head. In the end they got a rope and bound the pot firmly on Mr. Hyena's head tying the ends of the rope in a knot under his chin. They took Mrs. Pot home. When they arrived, they tried to put down the pot but failed. She frustrated them by getting stuck on Mr. Hyena's head. No matter how hard they pulled, she did not come off Mr. Hyena tried an alternative. He instructed his wife to use a pestleto knock off the pot from his head. Mrs. Hyena was dexterous. Sheaimed closely and hit hard. The pot quickly moved but letting the pestle land on Mr. Hyena's forehead. The blow caused a nasty wound. Blood was oozing out. The pot was still firmly on Mr. Hyena's head.His wife ran out to get some fresh leaves to stop the bleeding. She wiped off the blood and plastered the wound with them. She then bound the wound with a cotton cloth to keep the leaves in place.

The couple then decided that they must do something about the pot before they went to bed. They sneaked out and headed to the cashew tree. As they approached, Mr. Hyena ran with speed and aimed to knock off the pot against the tree. The pot swiftly moved to the back of the head. Bravely, Mr. Hyena pushed it irritatingly to the middle and tried again. The attempt failed. The pot kept on moving to avoid being knocked against the tree. Tired, frustrated and in pain, Mr. Hyena decided to go home with his wife. On arrival, Mrs. Hyena abandoned efforts to remove the pot. Instead, she took a big cotton cloth and secured the pot in place. They spent an uncomfortable and sleepless night.

Mr. Hare woke up early the next morning. He met Mrs. Hyena in the open area in front of the compound and enquired about Mr. Hyena. She told him that her husband was still sleeping. He had not been feeling well. With such a reason, Mr. Hare felt he should not disturb his friend. He therefore left for his farm.

Around midday, Mr. Hare sang the song for Mrs. Pot to bring the food. She did not come. He was puzzled. In the evening again, he sang so that Mrs. Pot would come with the food. She did not appear. He was disturbed. He wondered whether harm had gone her way. He went home very hungry.

On arrival, he remembered that he had not seen his friend lately. He met Mrs. Hyena by their entrance and said he wanted to see her husband. She said that he had gone to bed. Mr. Hare became suspicious. It was apparent that she was shielding him from visitors. To her, his appearance was too painful and unbearable.

Mr. Hare became determined to see his friend. He didn't know why Mr. Hyena had withdrawn.

Rumours were rife that his head had grown big and disfigured. He could not confirm that. He began to feel suspicious. Disfigured head and disappearance of his closest friend! The coincidence was curious. Only the two of them, Mr. Hyena and Mr. Hare knew about Mrs. Pot. He, Mr. Hare had not seen Mrs. Pot for a long time. She had not been responding to his song. He would watch Mrs. Hyena's movements closely. If she left their living area, he would sneak into his friend's living quarters to see him.

Mr. Hare immediately commenced his vigil of his friend's quarters. It was a wise move. He hit luck. Two hours after asking for his friend, he heard Mrs. Hyena discretely going out. He waited for ten minutes and went quietly to see Mr. Hyena. He was sitting down and leaning his head on the wall. On top of his head sat Mrs. Pot. Hyena's neck was swollen apparently from the weight. A piece of cloth was next to him on the floor.

Mr. Hare, with great difficulty suppressed a laugh. He could see why Mrs. Hyena did not want anyone to see her husband. He was an ugly sight. He looked hideous with the pot stuck on his head. Greed at its highest level had landed him in a pitiful situation. As soon as Mr. Hyena saw his friend, he turned his face away. He was ashamed of himself. Mr. Hare felt he had to speak and accusingly said:

"Well, my friend, you have betrayed my trust. You promised you would only call Mrs. Pot when you're in dire need of food. Were you in such a situation? If you had nothing to hide why did you keep away from me?"

Mr. Hyena did not look at Mr. Hare. He spoke but his voice was tight with pain:

"My dear friend, I'm really sorry. I didn't mean to treat you this way. I enjoyed Mrs. Pot's food and brought some home for my wife. We both got dependent on the free lunch. We were ashamed that you'd find out. So, I decided that the pot should be kept in my home. My wife helped me to put it on my head after many strenuous efforts. When we finally succeeded, our problems started. Mrs. Pot refused to descend from her position on my head. I've used a pestle to remove her but I failed. I tried to knock her off against the cashew tree. I failed again. Now ashamedly, I have to turn to you for mercy. Can you help me get her off? She is loyal to you. Please talk to her. I know she would respond. I'm exhausted and need a release."

Mr. Hare had to control himself. His friend looked like an orgy with Mrs. Pot securely perched on his head. Mr. Hare then explained:

"You see my friend, this is not an ordinary pot. It has special powers. You angered the spirits that are the source of the powers by removing Mrs. Pot from the magical place. It is unfortunate that you had to pay so dearly for your action. I believe that you have suffered enough. You should be helped. There is a way. You must appease the spirits by offering a sacrifice. The sacrifice is a white fowl that must be offered to the spirits under the silk cotton tree at the outskirts of this area. Mrs. Pot would automatically leave her seat on your head as would be willed by the spirits. However, let me make one point clear. You won't be allowed to taste even a piece of that fowl. You have wronged the spirits. You need to be cleared. Let me know as soon as you have the fowl. We'll go together to administer the sacrifice."

"I'll tell my wife to go out hunting for food very early tomorrow so that we can carry out the sacrifice quickly. Thank you so much for giving me the solution."

Hare left saying to himself: Mr. Hyena is fond of betraying his friends. I hope that this is a lesson he wouldn't forget. With these thoughts he retired for the night satisfied that he had at last located Mrs. Pot. He was awakened by Mrs. Hyena's voice. Excitedly she declared:

"I've got the fowl, I've got the fowl. Please wake up, Mr. Hare. My husband can no longer carry his head. He's complaining of severe headache. If you don't help us, he'll die."

Mr. Hare got up and went to his friend's quarters. Mr. Hyena took the fowl from his wife and handed it over to his friend. They walked out shoulder to shoulder as in old times into the deep part of the forest. When they reached the silk cotton tree, Mr. Hare went to the trunk of the tree, recited some words and killed the fowl.

He sprinkled some of the blood at the tree trunk and the rest on Mr. Hyena's head. There was a big rumbling as if a thunderstorm was imminent. A strong sandy whirl moved towards them. It almost swept them off their feet. They were temporarily blinded. When everything started to clear, they saw Mrs. Pot on the ground. She had descended. The spirits demonstrated their power. They cooked the fowl. When the food was ready, Mr. Hare settled down to eat. Mr. Hyena watched licking his tongue as his friend devoured everything. Mr. Hyena went home hungry. It was a painful lesson.

Chapter Eight

The bird and the lion fight for a beautiful girl

Once upon a time there was a small sparsely populated village known as Tellum. This village, because of its location was blessed with unusual heavy rainfall during the wet season. The rainfall was suitable for many crops that were cultivated by the people. Furthermore, the rains had a marvelous impact on the vegetation and ecosystem. Thick plant growth covered areas between the trees. It was not surprising that at the outskirts of the village were the big and very healthy plants in the farms. They were all green and the scenery was beautiful with different species of plants and habited by many types of animals, birds and insects. The palm trees were unusually tall, towering majestically over the large expanse of the fully cultivated rice fields and banana plantations in the lowlands. Mango, orange, coconut, medicinal, and wild trees naturally decorated the high lands. Beyond this rich cultivable area was the forest that occupied the hem of the farms. The forest was thick and grassy and had many and various trees standing close to each other. The environment was undoubtedly rich, natural and untouched. It was well preserved. Different types and sizes of animals that made the forest their home lived in harmony. Birds and insects were not absent. They were beautiful with rare colours. They fleeted playfully from tree to tree demonstrating their contribution to the beautiful habitat.

Tellum had another compliment to its natural beauty. In this place lived a beautiful, teenage girl named Asino. She was an only child to her mother, Nyajena and her father, Jalintora. Asino was mild-mannered and very dutiful. She had great respect for the elderly and was always ready to help anyone in need. She woke up very early every morning to get water from the village well for her parents to take their bath. She would quickly light a fire to heat the leftover rice from the previous day's supper to serve as the family breakfast. She ate with her parents before they set out for the day's work at the rice and groundnut farms.

At the farm Jalintora cleared the farm whilst Nyajena and Asino did the sowing of the seeds. This was their daily routine until the crops started to sprout up. Then as customary among the people of the village, the ladies would add a new feature to their work on certain days. They would go to the forest on those days to gather dry leaves. These leaves were dried further and later burnt. Their ashes would then be sprinkled on the growing plants. They believed that this would enrich the soil and so help the plants to develop healthily. Many times, Asino went with her mother, Nyajena and other women to gather dried leaves for their farms. They also got firewood to cook their meals.

Asino's name spread far. This was so because she was one of the very few girls who habitually worked side by side with her mother at the family farm. Some of her other companions were happy with tendering their young siblings. Perhaps her status as an only child deprived her from the responsibility of childcare. But then there was another girl who was the youngest in her family. She too had no siblings to take care of. Yet she was not as helpful to her mother as Asino. The girl was too lazy and scarcely went to the farm to help her parents. Thus Asino was greatly appreciated and treated as special. Her adorable qualities endeared her to her neighbours. Her good name reached animals and birds of the forest.

In the village's vicinity lived a bird named Kabarr Labatch. He was black in colour. He had a lengthy black beak and very long black tail. He was outgoing and easily made friends. His type of bird was frequently seen during the rainy season. Kabarr Labatch was fond of watching the women whilst busy at work. He hovered around very low especially when the women were very engaged in the gathering of dried leaves and firewood. He loved to listen to their gossips.

At moments of boredom, he would go to the farm to playfully try to steal some of the leaves they had gathered. He did this to tease and also attract their attention. Some of the young girls would occasionally run after him and throw small sticks at him. He would fly away at higher height only to swoop down again later just to be chased by the girls. He really enjoyed these playful moments. It was during such adventures that he came to notice Asino's striking beauty and got attracted. She was one of the girls who ran after him when he flew low to snatch away the dry leaves they had gathered.

The people of Tellum were very careful not to tamper with nature. They did not fell the trees for their firewood. They loved and respected their natural habitat and as such only used dead trees and dry sticks shed off by the healthy trees for their daily needs.

Thus the animal kingdom was likewise undisturbed. There was peaceful co-existence in that locality. The animals in the area were frequently within view of the people. They were never aggressive. They neither attacked nor scared away the human beings. Instead, they would hide behind trees to listen to their banter and watch them toil tirelessly on their farmland. The animals would later in their evening gatherings discuss about the complicated lives of their human neighbours. They wondered why human beings should complicate their lives with cooking food, building shelter and going through a difficult process of childcare and rearing.

The women of Tellum fascinated Mr. Lion the most. He enjoyed watching them from a distance when they were at their farms. He would lie under a big shady tree within hearing and seeing distances. He would spend his time quietly observing their every movement. It was during one of these periods that he got to recognize a young girl who constantly worked by another woman's side. He figured out that the two were mother and daughter, as they looked alike. They seemed to be very close. They chatted and laughed quietly. They enjoyed each other's company.

Mr. Lion closely studied the relationship between these two females. He admired the way they related to each other. The more he watched them from his hidden position the fonder he became of the young girl.

However, conscious of his physical appearance, he was apprehensive about his looks. He was known as a big fearful and wild animal. Many human beings were fearful of such animals. They did whatever they could in order to avoid coming face to face with them. Therefore, many of his kind would find him unrealistic to entertain the thought that a human being would fall in love with him. Nevertheless, with his feelings so strong Mr. Lion did not give up his dream. He could not resist the urge to go to the tree every day just to catch a glimpse of the girl whom he found so irresistible. The girl was called Asino.

Kabarr Labatch, the black bird too was also in a similar precarious situation. He was deeply in love with the same beautiful young girl. He frequented the farming area of the people of Tellum. He was there daily to tease the girls by picking on the grains and dry leaves that were available and then flying away. He was very observant. He recognised the fact that whenever he was in the vicinity of the farms of the people of Tellum, he would catch a glimpse of Mr. Lion lying under a tree within view. He noticed the longing in the eyes of Mr. Lion as he quietly followed the movements of the women. Kabarr Labatch erroneously thought that Mr. Lion was planning to catch one of the women for his dinner one fine day. Curious about Mr. Lion's strange conduct, Kabarr Labatch bravely approached him under the tree and said:

"Good day, Mr. Lion. What brings you here? You seem to like this spot under the tree. Is this your hideout for a siesta? If that's the case, I might as well not disturb you. I'm quite sure you need your space for a good chill out. I believe that it's good to chill out at times."

"Oh, who is that? The voice sounds like that of Kabarr Labatch? Is that his voice? If so, come! I'm just taking a short rest. I come here when I want to be on my own. Right now, I don't mind having some company.

Lately I've been idling. I like to watch the women working so hard for a living. I've always wondered whether I can ever make such great efforts to obtain food," replied Mr. Lion.

Kabarr Labatch paused thoughtfully and then cautiously opined:

"I know. These women are very hardworking. They work communally in order to finish what they have to do quickly. I fully understand that working as a group has its advantages. One of them is that they do not feel tired quickly. They therefore do not need long pauses as rest period."

"Hum, that's where they are different from us, animals. I do like their lifestyle. We can learn from them. For example, look at the admirable way that girl called Asino helps her mother. She's so dutiful. She's also very attractive. I like her. I wish I can make her my wife." Mr. Lion stated wishfully.

Kabarr Labatch suppressed a cynical but unhappy laugh. Mr. Lion's last statement angered him. He too, has been nursing the same thoughts about Asino for some time. He prudently did not reveal his feeling to Mr. Lion. He had to avoid irritating a strong and fierce animal like Mr. Lion. Depending on the temperature of the chat, he would cautiously make his feelings for Asino known a bit later. Continuing their chat, Kabarr Labatch commented:

"People are different. Have you noticed something about the people of Tellum? The men do the difficult part of farm work whilst the women enjoy lighter tasks. Their daughters go to the farm to play and take care of their younger siblings whilst their mothers were at work. I like their division of labour. If I was human, I'll be a woman.

"I didn't think of it in that way," Mr. Lion confessed.

"Well, I've played and interacted with these people for some time. I've also followed the behaviour of the girl Asino. She's gorgeous and admirable for she's very devoted to her mother. I believe that I've fallen in love with her," Kabarr Labatch revealed.

"Keep your hands off my girl!" Mr. Lion growled ferociously. His eyes turned red with the anger. A friend in whom he had confided about his feelings had betrayed him. Mr. Lion was not going to easily give up the girl. Kabarr Labatch had inadvertently sewn the seeds of discord. His declaration of love for the same girl was bound to bring friction between them. In one-way or the other, they would have to compete for her hand in the not too distant future. Lion was the first to put up the challenge.

"It seems that we would have to fight for Asino's hand. The earlier we do it the better. Whoever is the winner would approach her. The loser would have to stay away."

"It's a deal. However, the deal won't be between the two of us alone. We might have to establish the real winner by mobilizing all our friends. They would constitute our armies for the fight for Asino. They would be real armies." Kabarr Labatch argued.

"Alright. I'll bring all the wild animals of the forest to form my army in this big fight," Mr. Lion declared.

"Okay, I'll come with all the birds and anything that has wings. Flies, wasps, mosquitoes, all of them will be part of my army," countered Kabarr Labatch.

"In that case, all four legged tame and wild animals will be part of my army. I'll mobilise stray domestic animals such as cats, dogs, horses, pigs, donkeys, sheep and goats. You'll recognise that my constituency is bigger and more formidable than yours," declared Mr. Lion. Kabarr Labatch and Mr. Lion agreed to meet with their forces in three days' time. The fight would be held in an open area in the forest. Kabarr Labatch took one of his feathers as a flag and placed it firmly on the ground. Mr. Lion took one of his long strong whiskers, placed it upright on the ground as his own flag. The battle lines were thus drawn and their forces identified.

Mr. Lion went back to the forest, very confident. He knew that he had fierce animals such as Mr. Tiger and Mr. Hyena within his army. The domestic animals had always roamed freely in the forest because they regarded Mr. Lion as king of the forest. A relationship with them had been nurtured and Mr. Lion felt he could rely on them. He was therefore sure of a bigger fighting force compared to Kabarr Labatch. He would easily teach Kabarr Labatch and his army of flying species a lesson. This rival of his was a small weak bird and oblivious of his limitations was daringly challenging the mighty king of the forest.

The two rivals worked hard to prepare their forces. Mr. Lion summoned a meeting of all four legged animals. Elephants, lions, tigers, hyenas, giraffes, monkeys, baboons, antelopes, hares, goats, cattle, sheep, dogs, cats, pigs, horses and donkeys attended. They were all curious to know the purpose of the gathering. It was very unusual for Mr. Lion to ask them to assemble without prior notice.

The beat of the drum was heard but surprisingly a messenger did not precede it. Thus they realised that his call was urgent. All the animals therefore treated the call as an emergency. They regarded Mr. Lion as a good and very protective leader to them especially in their hours of need. They must reciprocate and go out in their numbers to answer his call. It was indeed an emergency meeting. Mr. Lion was there before all of them. He wasted no time to broach the subject.

"My dear citizens I know that you've all been wondering why I summoned you to an emergency meeting. I have done this because of the exceptional nature of the matter. Fellow citizens, this meeting is being summoned as a result of my decision to get a partner. In fact, I've already chosen one although I've not yet expressed my feelings to her. You might be wondering who she is. I must say that she is not one of us. Her name is Asino. She's human. She lives not far from here in Tellum." Mr. Lion paused. The animals looked at each other in utter disbelief. What? Mr. Lion was in love with a human being. He can't be serious. How could he think that a girl would marry a wild animal? They were amazed but cleverly kept their feelings to themselves until he finished his story. Mr. Lion resumed speaking:

"I have been watching this beautiful young girl, Asino and her mother, Nyajena at their family farm daily for more than three months. What is obviously noticeable is that the girl is very caring and dutiful to her mother. I liked this virtue in her. But what is painful is I didn't realize that I had a competitor. Today, I met Kabarr Labatch at the outskirts of the farms. We talked about a lot of things until our gossip drifted to Asino. Flippantly I disclosed my feelings for Asino to him. Later in the conversation, he too pronounced his interest in the same girl. Conflict of interest caused an argument over who should be the first to approach her to declare his love. We couldn't reach an agreement. Consequently, we decided to resolve the matter through a fight. It would not be determined on the basis of a one to one encounter.

Each would demonstrate his power also by mobilising from his kind. Kabarr Labatch would bring all flying birds and insects whilst I would bring all four legged animals. The encounter is in three days' time. The winner would emerge as the only suitor. I've therefore called you here to get volunteers for the fight against Kabarr Labatch and his army."

The animals were angry. They could not believe that small birds were willing to challenge them. Mr. Tiger, unable to hide his feeling asked to speak. He voiced the concern of all the other animals:

"What if Asino doesn't accept the winner. She's a human being. She wouldn't entertain marrying outside her kind." This thought had been uppermost in the minds of the other animals. They were silent. Mr. Lion was undaunted. He continued:

"Don't worry. We'll get over that hurdle when we come to it. First things should be done first. Let's deal with combatting a potentially formidable enemy."

All the animals whether in agreement or not nodded in unison. They were interested in fighting for their king. Each and every one of them wanted to be part of the army. They felt hurt a bird such as Kabarr Labatch would have the cheek to challenge the animals of the area.

They were determined to teach him humility. They would exert such attacks that the birds and insects would retreat on the very first encounter and within a very short engagement in battle. Mr. Hyena was assigned the role of leader of the battalion. He would give the command to fight by bellowing the words:

'Futique,' meaning 'attack'. In the event he wanted to change their military strategy or retreat, if necessary he would shout out: 'Futique perto.' With these words, his whole army would cleverly leave the battlefield. The animals felt well prepared for a quick and victorious battle.

Likewise, Kabarr Labatch too called up a meeting of birds, bats and insects. He explained what had transpired between himself and Mr. Lion, king of the animals. Kabarr Labatch and Mr. Lion had found out in their chat that both of them were in love with a girl named Asino. It was obvious that both of them had deep feelings for her and must fight for her hand.

That meant that they were each to build an army for the battle. Amazingly, the girl in question was unaware of the love of both Kabarr Labatch and Mr. Lion and that their love warranted the impending fight. However the event would unravel when a winner emerged.

Kabarr Labatch further explained that he felt insulted by Mr. Lion's haughty attitude towards all living things with wings. Thus the fight was a means of establishing the mightiest, the wisest and cleverest among non-humans. Kabarr Labatch in his explanation touched the emotions of his listeners. The birds, bats and insects felt belittled by Mr. Lion. They were bent on showing the animals that despite their small sizes they were a formidable force.

On the day of the battle, Kabarr Labatch sent an advance party comprising of bees, wasps, mosquitoes and other stinging insects. They left in good time with a lot of noise as they flew towards the arena. Mr. Lion saw them flying low and recognised that Kabarr Labatch's army was too small. So he decided that he did not require his full force on the battle line. He thus consulted the experienced animals and as a result quickly revised their plan. Their strategy was that Mr. Hyena would lead assisted by Mr. Hare. The other small animals such as the goats, sheep, cattle, pigs, monkeys, horses, donkeys, cats and dogs would follow. These animals would form the necessary force to easily squash Kabarr Labatch's small army.

The insects and bats entered the arena with their lots of loud and varied noises. The small animals mistook the loud buzzing noise as Mr. Hyena giving the command: 'futique!' They fiercely advanced to take on the insects.

The wasps and mosquitos tactically flew very low. They descended on the backs of Mr. Hyena, Mr. Hare and the other small animals. The insects buzzed as they settled on the ears and backs of the animals to sting and suck their blood. The animals were in great pain. The insect stings were as effective as deep pricks of red-hot needles. The animals had presumed that the fight would be on the ground. The use of wings to move about in the battlefield was never taken into consideration. Thus they were taken by surprise. It was imperative that they must reconsider their offensive move. With the insects' attack, Mr. Hyena, the leader shouted: ' futique perto.' The apparent retreat by the animals sent the insects into a panic.

They thought that this was a strategy of the animals to lead them to the forest where they would be out numbered with the addition of the fiercest animals.

They acted quickly. They got off the animals and flew away with a loud flutter. They must report the animals' strategy to Kabarr Labatch. They required further consultations and if necessary come up with another attack plan.

The bats, birds and insects met with Kabarr Labatch. They narrated what had happened at the battlefield. They tried to decode Mr. Hyena's words to the animals before they left for the deep forest. They made a lot of guesses. They did not succeed. Yet they were resolved to continue the fight the following day. Kabarr Labatch would go with them but he would be invisible. He would be in their midst. All bats, birds and insects would go in full force and descend mercilessly on the animals. They would use whatever combat means they had at their disposal to hurt the big animals. The stinging and biting insects would sharpen their stinging tools whilst birds would blind the animals by aggressively flapping their wings and dropping hairy grains of coos into the eyes of their enemies. However, they were very mindful of the strengths and power of their opponents. Giraffe was so tall that he could reach unimaginable heights. Monkeys and baboons were very agile and fast in movement. Lions were capable of swift jumps and their attacks, tearing their preys to pieces. They needed safeguards in a fight with a formidable army.

All the animals moved to the arena on the second day. The big animals protected the small animals led by Mr. Lion with a circle. Mr. Hyena led his force closely followed by Mr. Giraffe. They charged aggressively. The animals' strategy was to first conquer the bats and birds, before they would move to tackle the weak insects. The battle was fierce. Mr. Giraffe used his height to his advantage and killed some birds. He succeeded in doing so before one of the birds was able to drop a lot of hairy grains of coos into his eyes. The infuriated Mr. Lion and his kindred jumped and attacked their enemies with vengeance. Mr. Lion's troops penetrated the ranks of Kabarr Labatch's army. Mr. Lion wanted to tear his competitor to pieces.

The fight between them was short. Mr. Lion sprang to catch the bird. He was not very careful in his movement. The bird dropped a grain of hairy coos that irritated Mr. Lion's eyes. He was temporarily blinded. He shook his head so that the coos would drop off his eyes. When he opened his eyes again, Kabarr Labatch was nowhere to be seen.

The raging battle

Elsewhere, the battle raged on. The bees and wasps fought very hard. Their ability to fly was a big advantage, which the animals could not overcome. They stung the animals very hard before flying away quickly. Those that were attacked were in acute pain. They slowed down to lick their wounds.

They wanted to retreat but that command was not forthcoming from Mr. Hyena. Mr. Hare was bleeding on both ears. He shouted to their leader: Mr. Hyena, 'futique wa?'

The commander replied: 'futique!'

The wounded animals were disappointed. However, they fought on although weakly. Mr. Giraffe, Mr. Lion and their kind attacked the birds and tore their unfortunate victims to pieces. On the other hand, the bees and wasps fought very hard. They stung the animals fiercely and indiscriminately. The birds had some victims too into whose eyes they succeeded to drop hairy coos grains.

Three bees and wasps decided that the battle had raged long enough. They headed for the commander of the animals. They stung Mr. Hyena's ears but he proved brave and persevered with the fight. He was determined that the small flying insects and birds would never overcome the big and mighty animals. He was bent on forcing them to retreat first. If this did not happen, the fight would go on as long as possible. Despite the repeated questions from the wounded animals for a retreat, Mr. Hyena ignored the calls of his colleagues and continued to shout: 'futique!' When he uttered those words for the seventh time, six bees and wasps descended on him with full force. They reinforced the first group of attackers on the commander. They stung and bit his ears and nose. Blood gushed out. He felt dizzy and lost control of himself. He ceased to be aware of his actions. He suddenly cried out: 'futique perto!' On that pronouncement, all the animals took to their heels and ran with high speed towards the deep forest. The birds and insects followed them for some distance to ensure that the enemy was in retreat. They were the winners of this hard fought battle. The animals never returned to the battlefield. Victorious Kabarr Labatch was crowned King of the Birds. Being the victor of the battle secured him

both the heart and hand of the beautiful maiden,
Asino.

Chapter Nine

The six children of the World

Long ago, the world was just bare land and water. It was a small round ball. There was no living creature on it. Then something happened. The small round ball started to grow big. With this growth it was noticed that the day became shorter. Strangely too, the sun got covered most of the time. This affected the nights, which became longer. For most of these nights, the moon was partially covered.

The shape of this round ball changed. Its growth was greater around its middle than anywhere else. The outer harder skin expanded so much that the object increased to twice its former size. Side by side with the outward growth was a similar development inside. The growth inside was that of a huge activity. The walls inside produced an object. As this object grew in size, it cracked and divided into six equal parts. These six objects continued to grow and live inside the ball.

The shape, the size and the signals coming out of the ball pointed that it was the planet Earth. As some strange things happened, it seemed that the ball was about to define its existence. Things happened at an extraordinary rate. Every part of the ball or the Earth grew almost a million fold. Its size became vast. The limit of growth was reached and something had to give way.

A dull and cloudy day dawned. Fifteen hours after sunrise, there was a thunderous explosion. What a great big noise! The ground shook massively. It was awesome. It must be that the Earth had burst open. The contents poured on to the ground. What were they? Creatures of various size lay still on the ground. It would take time for what gushed out from the inside of the Earth to be characterised. It seemed that the beginning of human life was lying still on the ground.

First human beings were born

These things remained still on the ground although the stillness was not to last. The things were of different sizes with the smallest one being three metres long on the ground. They were bigger than the human beings that followed later. However, they had the features of human beings. They seemed to be fast asleep. They were breathing. Gentle movement replaced the stillness.

The living things were enormous creatures. They were gigantic. They had the ability to move and looked like huge human beings. They were very tall and had enormous muscles. They had four long limbs. The lower limbs, the legs were long and covered with a lot of hair. There were five toes on each foot. The upper limbs, the hands were long and very muscular. They were however shorter than the legs. They were covered with short fairly distributed hair. Each hand had five fingers of different sizes.

The creatures had big and round heads with a lot of thick long hair falling down from them to their shoulders. Each head had two big round bulging eyes. Their faces were of different shapes: long, oval, short and round. They carried long noses with fan-like ends that housed the nostrils. The mouths were not outdone in size. They had to be big and very wide. The noise that came from their mouths was very loud blowing away the sand near where they laid. When they moved their limbs slightly, they opened their big bulging eyes very wide.

As they lay down lazily on the ground, all six of them clenched their hands as if holding on to something. They moved their hands slightly when they wanted to change their positions. All of them did not wear clothes. Yet they were not ashamed. These creatures were the first human beings brought forth on earth.

They were evenly distributed: three males and three females. The females were called Khorma, Saye and Sutuurah. The males were known as Baarkeh, Woorsak and Haarit. Their names symbolised the important values of life.

One glorious morning as the early sun glittered through the still air, Baarkeh slowly and with great effort, sat up. He stretched out his hands on the ground. The experience was amazing. A strange sensation crept into his limbs. The feeling grew stronger and developed into energy. The urge to be more daring pushed him to move one step towards where Khorma lay lazily. She stared in wonderment. Baarkeh walked unsteadily to her.

"Come along. Give it a go. I'll help you," cried out Baarkeh in excitement.

"I'm afraid. Hold my hand. You know we've never done this before," Khorma stammered as she stretched out her right hand. Baarkeh grabbed the hand with a tight grip. He pulled her upwards gently to her feet. He held on to her hand. Khorma swayed dizzily. She shut her eyes. When she opened them she felt steady. Slowly, she picked her shaky steps.

She tottered to the side of Baarkeh and stood next to him. The other siblings watched them in wonder and amazement. This was a formidable achievement. The faces of the others betrayed their curiosity and interest to try this new spectacle.

The others were inspired. They wanted to learn what Baarkeh and Khorma had done. Who would be bold enough to make a move? They all made some weak attempts. Saye was the boldest. She bravely knelt down. It was painful. She twitched her eyebrows. She was determined that she was not going to be stopped by that hurt. In a snail's pace, she shakily lifted herself and stood up. She felt dizzy and almost fell down. She closed her eyes and remained still. When she opened her eyes, the dizziness was gone. She was steady.

As she resumed her measured steps, she looked to the right and noticed that Woorsak was trying to stand up. Woorsak was the heaviest of all of them. she moved to him and held his hand. Inch by painstaking inch, Woorsak stood up. He took careful step after step like a baby learning to walk.

Sutuurah and Haarit were encouraged. Their other siblings were going through a fantastic experience. They must try it. They found it easier to move because of their light built. The support they gave to each other was reassuring. They gradually learnt to move together. Speed in movement grew quickly. Walking around was easier and more frequent. The urge to explore their surrounding became very pressing. They had formed pairs. As pairs, therefore, they moved and walked together.

The ability to move quickly encouraged the siblings to explore their surroundings. They knew they must find out about their environment. The short, tough grasses on the ground were crushed under their heavy feet. They were huge. They towered over trees. It was quite easy for them to pluck fruits from the trees to eat in order to satisfy their hunger. Fresh drinking water was not easy to find. They had to walk for long distances to get tp water to quench their thirst. Life on earth was very exciting to them.

The companionship that the siblings forged among themselves flourished. It grew into partnerships. As a result, the seeds of emotional relationship between male and female were sown. The partnerships grew and produced children. Thus procreation started. The human race was guaranteed of continuation for years to come.

Haarit and Sutuurah had the most productive partnership. They had fifteen children. Their first child was born two years after they started living together. The child brought them closer together. They enjoyed parenthood. Thus they had their children in shor intervals.

The frequency of childbirths harmed Sutuurah's health and looks. Yet she continued to have another child, her sixteenth. She did not survive it. The baby, a daughter, was given the name, Khorma. Haarit named her after his favourite sister. He doted on her. Perhaps he did this because the child looked very much like her mother. Another reason could have been that the baby would enjoy the love of a mother. No one knew why Haarit over indulged on Baby Khorma.

The presence of Baby Khorma and the joy of having her did not completely wipe out Haarit's grief. He was devastated by the death of his loving partner. Sadness darkened his eyes. He would gaze in space with the feeling of being desolate. The other siblings got worried. They realised that it was very crucial to save him. Baby Khorma and her siblings needed a parent alive.

The group entrusted the responsibility of consoling their bereaved brother to Baarkeh. He was the most sympathetic among them all. He took the duty bestowed on him seriously. He knew that Haarit was very proud and could reject pity in any form. Thus he had to be subtle. Baarkeh therefore wisely directed his daily visits to the children. The children got attached to him. Through them he was able to touch his brother's life.

With time, Haarit began to get accustomed to his brother's visit. He always looked forward to his companionship. He grew anxious when his brother failed to turn up. When such occasions arose, he would encourage his children to walk with him to check on 'Papa Baarkeh'. Life gradually became meaningful again.

Haarit really appreciated the support of Baarkeh. They spent a lot of time together. This helped Baarkeh who was an outdoor person to learn to stay indoors. Staying indoors though was not to last long. Soon Baarkeh resumed his adventurous life. He was an explorer. He loved to go outside their living area to search for food and learn more about his environment. One fateful day, he ventured out on his many solitary walks. He felt that the weather was pleasant and so he could go for a long distance in search of food. He knew the area very well.

That day, Baarkeh was in a very pensive mood. He did not pay much attention to where he was going. He soon took an unfamiliar path. He wasn't aware that he was walking on very marshy ground. The walk was not easy. Yet he did not try to find out what was pulling him down. He would carelessly struggle to lift his feet out. When he resumed his difficult steps, his feet would sink into the ground.

During one of such struggles to free his feet, he sank even deeper. It was then that he realised that he was in the middle of an expansive marsh. He was horrified. Panic followed. He was alone. He had nothing to hold on to for support. His masculine pride over-powered him. He thought to himself: I'll never cry for help. I'm strong and big enough to pull myself out.

Baarkeh resolved to struggle no matter how long it took him to succeed. Luck was not on his side. The more effort he made to get out, the deeper his giant feet sank. His huge size was a handicap. Slowly he lost his strength. He got tired and weakened. His desperate state led him to overcome his pride. Baarkeh screamed out loudly for help. The screams echoed. No one heard and came. The more he struggled and screamed, the deeper he sank. The marsh closed around him. Breathing became difficult even though he courageously fought for his life. He was overpowered. He died in a losing battle.

Baarkeh's wife, Khorma waited for days. It was a tortuous period. He did not appear. Hope that her husband was safe gradually disappeared with every passing day. The very long days went on to weeks. Distraught took over from the quiet calm comportment.

She became anxious and went through many sleepless nights. Her children got impatient and irritable. They tormented her about going out to get their father. Helpless, Khorma decided to confide in Haarit about Baarkeh's disappearance. Haarit was shocked by the dreadful news about Baarkeh. He tried to comfort her by reassuring her that he was safe. He felt that his brother would soon come back. He was adventurous and must have walked too far away. Deep in his heart, though Haarit was in despair. Despite the fact that he tried to mask it, Khorma was too intelligent to be deceived. She was not convinced by Haarit's consoling words. Besides, she had sensed his deeper feelings. Disheartened and helpless she went home. She cried day and night. Her hope for her partner's return was fading.

One day Haarit paid her a visit. It had been quite some time since they met. He was afraid that Khorma had given up on her partner. In such a circumstance, she might degenerate to a state of being helpless and dejected. Haarit himself did not know what to do. He was still anxious over the weird lack of news from Baarkeh.

As Haarit approached the compound his heart started to race. What was he hearing? Was that a moan? He wondered. He involuntarily quickened his pace. Fear got the better of him. His lower limbs weakened. He became slower in his movement. He staggered as he attempted to reach the eldest child near the gate. He signalled to him to go nearer to him. He then addressed him in a whisper:

"What is the matter? Why are you crying? Where is your mother?"

The child could not answer. With his eyes he said everything. He pointed his forefinger towards a room. Haarit walked into the compound. All the children were crying. He hesitated. Haarit was afraid to go further. He then mustered enough courage to go towards the direction of the room. Using the wall as his support, Haarit slowly and with great difficulty entered the room. His worse fears were confirmed. Khorma was heartbroken. She could not bear the disappearance of her partner. She took her life during the night in order to be with Baarkeh. What a big loss for the family! The children had become orphans within a very short period.

The first children of the Earth had already lost three members, Sutuurah, Baarkeh and Khorma. Their number had reduced. There were only three survivors: Saye, Haarit and Woorsak. Unfortunately, the three of them were not close to each other. Thus their children likewise did not interact. They had nothing to do with each other. The family structure started to disintegrate.

Space started to become a problem as all the siblings and their children continued to multiply. Consequently, the children and grandchildren of Khorma and Baarkeh decided to relocate. They went very far away and built their homes in a continent known as Africa. Some of the children of Sutuurah and Haarit also left the area. They built their new homes in a continent known as Asia. The other part of that family went to the north. This was a very cold place where the rain was icy. It was called Europe.

It is believed that this was how the human race multiplied and migrated to different places. When these first human beings separated, they unfortunately lost important traditional values. Faithfulness, blessings and trust disappeared with the deaths of Sutuurah, Baarkeh and Khorma. The institution of companionship became marriage (Saye). It has survived although it had not remained as strong as it was years ago. In some countries, the essence of marriage has lost a lot of value. Being true, loyal and faithful in any relationship has become a real challenge. Many people think about personal instead of the collective interest.

In olden times, it was believed that blessings (Baarkeh) begot good luck (Woorsak). Nowadays, luck is no longer associated with a divine gift. Values have changed. Materialism has made people believe that luck was personal. Greed has taken over from contentment. Everybody wants to be rich. People are no longer contented with meeting their basic needs. Today, they all want to be filthy rich. Even if rich, they fail to meet their humanitarian and family obligations.

Secrecy (Sutuurah) gave birth to friendship (Haarit). Friendship has survived. It has enjoyed an important place in people's lives. The virtue, though, is weakening. People no longer help the needy for humanitarian reasons. There are always strings attached to help. Many good deeds are publicised. Belief in humanity and privacy is fast disappearing.

The original human species carried the names of the basic values essential to the survival of humanity. Saye was the name given to that important institution that validated the union between a male and a female. This was the vehicle of growth of the human race. Sutuurah, Baarkeh and Haarit are acquired attributes. Contented human beings strive to acquire them.

Glossary

1. Khorma : this is a Wolloff word for an appreciative person
2. Saay: this is the Wolloff word for marriage
3. Barrkeh : this is a Wolloff word to describe a blessed person
4. Woorsak : this is the Wollof word for good luck
5. Sutuurah: this is a Wollof word that describes a person who keeps secrets
6. Haarit: this is the Wolloff word for a friend
7. Santang tree- The bark is used as incense
8. Lumo: weekly market day
9. Mbollohi mi: Members of the gathering (Wollof)
10. Nianyaa: breasts in Mandinka
11. Boppi Jerreh (Wollof), Jerreh Kungoto (Mandinka): this is the local name of Dog Island
12. Cheebu jen: rice cooked with fish and vegetables.
13. Maafeh: Groundnut stew
14. Soupa Kandia: Palm oil stew with okra
15. Njam: Tattoo
16. Taara: single woman living with her partner.
17. Fudan: Henna
18. Ndow rabin: this is a cultural event of the Lebou tribe of Senegal. Banjul Wollof used to

organise a late afternoon festival at the same time as Gamo Sabarr.

19.   Kunda: a clan living together
20. Seepah : roots that freshen the taste of water
21. Kenno : hard and solid white wood
22. Daara: Arabic school teaching religious education
23. Duurango: groundnut stew
24. Bolong: a tributary
25. Daharr: black tamarind
26. Findo: this is a cereal that is steamed and then served with stew.
27.   Kasumai: How are you? (Jola)
28. Kasumai kepp: Fine, thank you. (Jola).
29. Kalim dou Johla: the bush fowl that is between us.
30. Kabarr Labatch: the scientific name of African Pied Hornbill.
31. Futiq perto: This is the Jola word for 'to retreat'.
32. Futique wa: What sort of fight is this?
33. Futique! : This is the Jola command for 'fight'!
34. Jalang : shrine of the Jola tribe
35. Mbudakeh: this is dried coos made into Chereh and then pounded with sugar and groundnut paste.
36. Chourah gerteh: rice pounded with powdered groundnuts. It is cooked as a porridge.
37. Boom mi Beran Sirrah: the line demarcating the abode of the genii, Beran Sirrah.

38. Fanaal: this is a big boat shaped lantern made of soft bamboo and covered in intricate designs of paper filigree. It is paraded round the streets of the city of Banjul during Christmas.
39. Rulee Xutumba: this is the fanaal parade of children. It takes place during the day.
40. Novice: a person new to a field or activity.
41. Detour: a roundabout way.
42. Catapult: a slingshot.
43. Opportune: right for a particular occasion.
44. Conspiracy: an agreement to carry out an unlawful act.
45. Marksmanship: a man skilled in shooting at a target.
46. Adept: very skilled.
47. Congenial: sociable, agreeable.
48. Trample: to beat down with the feet in order to crush.
49. Annul: to make or declare invalid.
50. Maneuver: a controlled change in direction.
51. Ya ngeh chalit: you are overwhelmed.
52. Euphoria: a short feeling of happiness.
53. Magnanimity: nobel and generous.
54. Reciprocate: make a return for something given or done
55. Mesmerise: attract strongly.
56. Panic: fear.
57. Annul: to erase.
58. Resonate: to show a feeling of shared emotions.
59. Grand boubou: grown.

60. Energise: to give energy.
61. Hideous: revoltingly ugly.
62. Sine die: with no agreed date to meet again.
63. Muster: gather together.
64. Buoyant: engaged in much activity.
65. Reject: refuse to agree.
66. Siesta: an afternoon rest.
67. Treasure: very valuable.

About the Author

Sukai Mbye Bojang

Sukai Mbye Bojang is very interested in the tales of the different Gambian tribes. Her mother and late maternal grandmother had told her many stories as a child. As her grandmother grew old, she started to record them in 2003 with the intention of publishing them later. The stories were mainly from the Wollof and Mandinka tribes.

In 2008, Sukai enrolled for a Master's degree course at De Montfort University in Leicester in order to pursue a course in Creative Writing and New Media. During that period she collected more stories from the Fula tribe to add to the collection. She used her stories in the fiction course and submitted most of them for peer review and tutor assessment.

She co-authored two storybooks entitled Folk Tales and Fables of The Gambia Volume 1 in 2009 and then Folk Tales and Fables of The Gambia Volume 2 produced in 2010. Both books are used in the Gambian upper basic school system. This is the third volume in the series.